Sex In Every City

Sex
In Every City

How To Talk Dirty In Every Language

L. BROOK

MICHAEL O'MARA BOOKS LIMITED

The publishers would like to thank the following people
for their invaluable contributions to the compilation of this book:
Jane Carson, Athene Chanter, Rod Green, Llinos Roberts,
Ruth Shippobotham, Mauro Spagnol and Emily Vigliar.

First published in Great Britain in 2006 by
Michael O'Mara Books Limited
9 Lion Yard, Tremadoc Road
London SW4 7NQ

A CIP catalogue record for this book is available
from the British Library

ISBN (10 digit): 1-84317-196-1
ISBN (13 digit): 978-1-84317-196-6

1 3 5 7 9 10 8 6 4 2

www.mombooks.com

Designed and typeset by Martin Bristow

Translations by First Edition Translations Ltd, Cambridge, UK

Printed and bound in Great Britain
by Cox & Wyman, Reading, Berkshire

Contents

Introduction

Picture the scenario: you are a young, horny holidaymaker,
sampling the local nightlife. You're sunburnt, disoriented and
more than a little intoxicated. Approaching the bar, you spot
the lover of your dreams smiling engagingly in your direction.
Gazing at them seductively, you sidle over and open your mouth,
ready to utter the immortal line, 'Do you come here often . . .?'
– only to realize that the Italian stallion or Spanish sex bomb
won't understand a single word of your tried-and-tested routine.
So you resort instead to the universal language of love:
the primitive seduction dances and mating calls practised
by our pre-verbal ancestors. But rather than getting you laid,
it gets you a slap in the face and a fiery torrent of abuse.

Owners of this book need not worry about this hypothetical
situation, however. With every page featuring four essential
European languages – French, Spanish, Italian and German –
Sex In Every City also plays host to various exotic guest
languages. So next time you venture abroad, you can rest safe
in the knowledge that you will be able to pull in Portuguese,
fornicate in French, screw in Spanish, romp in Russian, hump in
Hindi, titillate in Thai and get down and dirty in Danish.
Including vocabulary and phrases to ease you through every
sexual situation – from making the crucial first move to getting
steamy in the bedroom, expressing post-coital satisfaction to
finding your way to the nearest STD clinic – this book has it all.
As if that wasn't enough, you can also amaze your lover(s) with
a variety of global sex facts and trivia, guaranteed to shock,
surprise and arouse in equal measure.

Enjoy having sex in every city.
Just remember to use protection.

L. BROOK, 2006

Basic Chat-up Lines

French
Tu viens ici souvent?
Too ve-en eesee soovon?

✳

Spanish
¿Viene aquí mucho?
Bee-eh-neh ah-kee moo-choh?

✳

Italian
Vieni spesso qui?
Veeay-nee spays-so kwee?

✳

German
Kommst du hier oft?
Komst doo heer offt?

✳

Swedish
Kommer du hit ofta?
Kommer dui heet ofta?

✳

Dutch
Kom je hier vaak?
Come yey hree vark?

✳

Portuguese
Você vem aqui muito?
Vos-eh veng ah-kee mwee-toh?

French
Alors, ça roule?
Alor, sa rool?

✳

Spanish
¿Qué tal?
Keh tal?

✳

Italian
Come stai?
Ko-may sta-ee?

✳

German
Wie geht's?
Vee gates?

✳

Danish
Hva' så der?
Va so dare?

Travellers' Tip

*If you are looking to get down
and dirty, head to Greece. The 2005
Durex Global Sex Survey confirmed that
Greece is officially the sexiest country with
the Greeks having sex 138 times a year –
well above the global average of 103.*

French
Salut, beau gosse!
Saloo, boh goss!

∗

Spanish
¡Hola, chato!
Oh-lah chah-toh!

∗

Italian
Ciao, bello!
Chaow bayl-lo!

∗

German
Hallo Matrose!
Hallo mat-rowzer!

∗

Finnish
No hyvää päivää!
No heuva paaiva!

Global Sex Fact

The most common universal form of marriage is polygyny (one husband with two or more wives). Anthropologist George Peter Murdock's Ethnographic Atlas claims that of 849 societies, 70 per cent are polygynous.

French
Il fait chaud ici, ou c'est juste toi?
Il fay show eesee, ou seh juste twah?

✳

Spanish
¿Hace calor aquí, o eres tú?
Ah-theh kah-lohr ah-kee, oh eh-rehs too?

✳

Italian
Fa caldo qui, o è perchè ci sei tu?
Fa kal-do kwi, o e payr-ke chee say too?

✳

German
Ist es hier warm, oder bist du nur heiß?
Ist ess here varm, oder bist doo nore hyse?

✳

Swedish
Är det varmt här eller, är det bara du?
Ar dier varmt har eller, ar de-et?

Global Sex Fact

In the eighteenth century many French brothels contained salles de préparations, *special rooms for the preparation of cosmetics, perfumes and aphrodisiacs.*

French
Ça te dirait de tirer un coup vite fait?
Sa tuh deeray duh teeray un coo veet fay?

Spanish
¿Hace un polvete?
Ah-theh oon pohl-veh-teh?

Italian
Che cosa ne diresti di una sveltina?
Kay ko-za nay dee-ray-stee dee oo-na svayl-tee-na?

German
Wie wäre es mit einem Quickie?
Vee vay-reuh es mit ine-em qfuickie?

Czech
Co takhle si dát rychlovku?
Tso takhle si daat rikhlofkoo?

Global Sex Fact

*A 'lingerie museum' in Hollywood
contains raunchy exhibits donated
by Cybill Shepherd, Madonna
and Zsa Zsa Gabor, among others.*

French

J'aimerais beaucoup me réveiller à côté de toi demain matin.

Jaimeray bohcoo muh revayay a coatay duh twah duhman matan.

✻

Spanish

Me encantaría despertarme junto a ti a la mañana siguiente.

Meh ehn-kahn-tah-ree-ah dehs-pehr-tahr-meh hoon-toh ah tee ah la mah-nee-ah-nah see-ghee-ehn-teh.

✻

Italian

Mi piacerebbe molto svegliarmi vicino a te domani mattina.

Mee pee-ache-rayb-bay mol-to svay-leear-mee vee-chee-no a tay do-ma-nee mat-tee-na.

✻

German

Ich möchte gerne morgen früh mit dir aufwachen.

Ish mersht-eh gurner morgan froo mit deer ouf-vacken.

✻

Russian

Я бы хотéл (*male speaker*) / хотéла (*female speaker*) проснýться зáвтра ýтром рядом с тобóй.

Ya bee hatel (male speaker) / hatela (female speaker) prasnootsa zavtra ootram riadam s taboy.

French
Sois sage!
Swah sahj!

✳

Spanish
¡Oh, pórtate bien!
Oh, pohr-tah-teh bee-ehn!

✳

Italian
Comportati bene!
Kom-por-tatee bay-nay!

✳

German
Dir geht's wohl zu gut.
Deer geht-s vohl tsoo goot.

✳

Russian
Эй, не шали́!
Hey, nie shali!

Global Sex Fact

On average, European women expect sex four times a week. This pales in comparison with Catherine the Great of Russia, who advocated sexual relations six times a day.

French

Tu me rends si nerveux / nerveuse que j'en oublie mes techniques de drague.

Too muh rond see nerv-euh / nerv-euse kuh jon ooblee may tekneek duh drag.

Spanish

Me has alterado tanto que ya me he olvidado completamente del rollo que me gasto para ligar.

Meh ahs ahl-teh-rah-doh tahn-toh keh yah meh eh ohl-bee-dah-doh kohm-pleh-tah-mehn-teh dehl rroh-yoh keh meh gahs-toh pah-rah lee-gahr.

Italian

Mi hai talmente agitato / agitata da farmi completamente dimenticare la frase che impiego abitualmente per abbordare qualcuno / qualcuna.

Mee aee tal-mayn-tay a-jee-tato / a-jee-tata da far-mee complay-tamayn-tay dee-mayn-tee-kaaray la fra-say kay eem-pye-go a-bee-tooal-mayn-tay payr ab-borda-ray kwal-koo-no / kwal-koo-na

German

**Du machst mich so nervös, dass ich meine übliche
Anmache ganz vergessen habe.**

Doo makhst mish so nerveus, das ish mye-neuh oobli-sheuh
anma-kheuh gants fergessen ha-beuh.

Hebrew

גרמת לי כזו התרגשות, ששכחתי לגמרי את משפט
הפתיחה הרגיל שלי.

Garamt li ca-zo hitragshut, she-shakhakhti le-gamrei
et mishpat ha-ptikha sheli.

Global Sex Facts

*Nine of the ten insular Pacific societies
condone sex before marriage.*

*Pendulous breasts are considered
so desirable among the Baganda that
young women are said to apply weights
to their breasts in order to achieve
the desired effect.*

✳

*Certain African cultures such as the Masai
practise puberty rituals which include
female circumcision.*

French
Je peux t'offrir un verre?
Juh peuh toffrear un vare?

✳

Spanish
¿Puedo comprarte una bebida?
Pweh-doh komp-rar-teh oon-ah beh-bee-dah?

✳

Italian
Posso offrirti qualcosa da bere?
Pos-so of-freer-tee kwal-koza da bay-ray?

✳

German
Kann ich dich auf ein Bier einladen?
Can ish dish ouf ine beer ine-larden?

✳

Swedish
Far jag bjuda dig pa en drink?
Fuor yaa biuda dei puo en drink?

✳

Welsh
Gai brynu diod i ti?
Gae brinoo deeodd ee tee?

✳

Korean
음료수 사 드릴까요?
Eum-ryo-soo sa deu-ril-ka-yo?

French
Pourquoi tu t'assieds pas à côté de moi?
Pourkwah too tasseeay paz a coatay duh mwah?

✳

Spanish
¿Porqué no te sientas aquí a mi lado?
Pohr-keh noh teh see-yen-tas ah-kee ah mee lah-doh?

✳

Italian
Perchè non ti siedi qui, vicino a me?
Payr-ke non tee see-ay-dee kwi, vee-chee-no a may?

✳

German
Warum setzt du dich nicht hier zu mir?
Varoom setst doo dish nisht heer tsu meer?

✳

Thai
ทำไมไม่นั่งข้างฉัน
Tam-mai mai nang khang chan?

Global Sex Fact

In Japan 'No-pan Kissa' are coffee shops containing mirrored floors designed to allow customers to look up waitresses' skirts.

French
T'as de beaux yeux, tu sais.
Ta duh boze yeuh, too say.

✳

Spanish
Tienes los ojos más lindos que he nunca visto.
Tee-eh-nehs lohs oh-hos mas lind-ohs keh eh noon-kah vees-toh.

✳

Italian
Hai i più bei occhi che abbia mai visto.
Aee ee peeyoo bay-ee ok-ee kay ab-beea maee vee-sto.

✳

German
Du hast die schönste Augen, die ich je gesehen habe.
Doo hass-t dee shurnst-eh owgen dee ish yay gezayen ha-beuh.

✳

Dutch
Zo'n mooie ogen heb ik nog nooit gezien.
Zoan moaye ogun heb ik nog noayt gezeen.

Global Sex Fact

A study in Australia showed that men who snore tend to have higher levels of testosterone.

French
Ta mère sait que tu es dehors aussi tard?
Ta mare say kuh too eh de-oar osee tar?

✳

Spanish
¿Tu madre sabe que estás fuera tan tarde?
Too mah-dreh sahb-eh keh ehs-tahs fu-er-ah tan tar-deh?

✳

Italian
Tua madre lo sa che sei fuori così tardi?
Too-a ma-dray lo sa ke say foo-oree ko-zi tar-dee?

✳

German
Weißt deine Mutter, dass du so spät raus bist?
Vice-t dye-ner mooter das doo so shpay-t rous biss-t?

✳

Danish
Ved din mor godt, du er ude så sent?
Ved din mor got, doo er oo so saint?

Global Sex Fact

The chastity belt is believed to have originated in the Middle East and been imported to medieval Italy, where it became known as the 'Florentine Girdle'.

'Get your coat, you've pulled.'

French
Va chercher ton manteau, tu as conclu.
Va shershay ton mantow, too a konkloo.

Spanish
Ponte el abrigo, que has ligado.
Pohn-teh ehl ah-bree-goh keh ahs lee-gah-doh.

Italian
Vai a prendere il cappotto, mi hai rimorchiato.
*Va-ee a prayn-day-ray eel kap-pot-to, mee aee
ree-morkeea-to.*

German
Hol deine Jacke, du hast das große Los gezogen.
*Hol dye-neuh yak-euh, doo hast das gross-euh los
getso-gen.*

Finnish
Sulla tais käydä flaksi.
Soolla tais kauda floksi.

Global Sex Fact

*In sixteenth-century Europe
one of the few acceptable reasons
for divorce was non-consummation.*

French
Tu plais à ma / mon pote.
Too play a ma / mon pot.

✻

Spanish
Mi amigo / amiga te gusta.
Mee ah-mee-goh / ah-mee-gah teh goos-tah.

✻

Italian
Piaci al mio amico / alla mia amica.
Peea-chee al mee-o amee-ko / al-la mee-a amee-ka.

✻

German
Mein Freund / Meine Freundin hier findet dich sehr sexy.
Mine froind / Mye-neuh froindin heer findet dish ser sexy.

✻

Czech
Líbíš se mému kamarádovi (male friend) /
kamarádce (female friend).
*Leebeesh seh memoo camaraadovi (male friend) /
camaraadtse (female friend).*

Global Sex Fact

*In some parts of New Guinea
pulling someone's penis is a gesture
of goodwill.*

French
Ça va, chéri/ chérie?
Sa va, sheree?

✳

Spanish
¿Qué tal, cielo?
Keh tahl, thee-eh-loh?

✳

Italian
Va bene, tesoro?
Va bay-nay, tay-soro?

✳

German
Alles klar, Süße?
Al-less klaar, zoo-sser?

✳

Russian
Все хорошó, дорогáя (*to a woman*) / дорогóй (*to a man*)?
Vsio harasho, daragaya (to a woman) / daragoy (to a man)?

✳

Portuguese
Tudo bem, querida?
Toodoo beng, keh-ree-dah?

Global Sex Fact

Fellatio is illegal in fifteen US States.

Advanced Chat-up Lines

'Have you ever been to the moon? Come and sit on my rocket and I'll take you there and back.'

French

Tu n'as jamais été sur la lune? Viens t'asseoir sur ma fusée et on fera l'aller-retour.

Too na jamay etay soor la loon? Ve-en tasswoir sur ma foozay ay on fera lallay ruhtour.

Spanish

¿Has estado en la luna? Ven a sentarte en mi cohete, que te doy un viaje de ida y vuelta.

Ahs ehs-tah-doh ehn la loo-nah? Behn ah sehn-tahr-teh ehn mee koh-eh-teh, keh teh doh-ee oon bee-ah-heh deh ee-dah ee boo-ehl-tah.

Italian

Sei mai stata sulla luna? Vieni a sederti sul mio razzo e ti ci porto.

Say ma-ee sta-ta sool-la loo-na? Veeay-nee a say-dayr-tee sool mee-o ra-tzo ay tee chee por-to.

German

Warst du schon einmal auf dem Mond? Komm und setz dich auf meine Rakete, ich bring dich dorthin und wieder zurück.

Varst doo shon ine-mal ouf dem mond? Kom oond sets dish ouf mye-neuh racket-euh, ish bring dish dorthin oond veeder tsooroock.

French

**Bon, si tu refuses de m'offrir un truc à boire,
je suppose qu' un p'tit coup dans le parking
est hors de question?**

Bon, see too refuse duh moffrear un trooc a bwoir,
juh suppose kun p'tee coo don luh parking
eh oar duh kesteeon?

✳

Spanish

**¡Vaya ¿Si no piensas invitarme
a una copa, supongo que un polvo
en el aparcamiento tampoco entrará
en tus planes?**

Bah-yah! See noh pee-ehn-sahs een-bee-tahr-meh
ah oo-nah koh-pah, soo-pohn-goh keh oon pohl-boh
ehn ehl ah-pahr-kah-mee-ehn-toh tahm-poh-koh ehn-trah
ehn toos plah-nehs?

✳

Italian

**Beh, se rifiuti di offrirmi qualcosa da bere,
suppongo che una sveltina nel parcheggio
è fuori discussione?**

Beh, say ree-fyou-tee dee of-freer-mee kwal-koza da bay-ray,
soop-pon-go ke oo-na svayl-tee-na nayl par-kay-jee-o
eh foo-o-ree dees-koos-seeo-nay?

Na, wenn du mir keinen Drink spendierst, ist auch kein Quickie auf dem Parkplatz drin, oder?

Na, ven doo meer kine-en drink shpendeerst, ist oukh kine qfuickie ouf dem parkplats drin, oder?

✳

Hindi

देखो, अगर तुम मेरे लिए ड्रिंक नहीं खरीदोगी तो पार्किंग में जाकर मैं तुम्हारी दूसरी प्यास नहीं बुझाऊंगा।

Male: Dekho, agar toom mere liye drink nahi khareedogi toe parking mein jaakar maen toomhaari doosri pyaas nahi boojhaoonga.

देखो, अगर तुम मेरे लिए ड्रिंक नहीं खरीदोगे तो पार्किंग में जाकर मैं तुम्हारी दूसरी प्यास नहीं बुझाऊंगी।

Female: Dekho, agar toom mere liye drink nahi khareedogei toe parking mein jaakar maen toomhaari doosri pyaas nahi boojhaoongi.

Travellers' Tip

If home videos are your thing, then head to the USA. Americans and Canadians lead the way for favouring sex in front of a camera.

French

Excuse-moi, tu crois aux aventures d'un soir?

Excuse-mwah, too crwah oze avontoor dun swoir?

∗

Spanish

Disculpa, ¿crees en amores de una noche?

Dees-kool-pah, kreh-ehs ehn ah-moh-rehs deh oo-na noh-che?

∗

Italian

Scusami, credi alle storie di una notte?

Skoo-za-mee, kre-dee al-lay sto-reeay dee oo-na not-tay?

∗

German

Entschuldigung, glaubst du an Sex für eine Nacht?

Entshooldigoong, gloubst doo an sex foor ine-euh nakht?

∗

Hindi

माफ कीजिए, क्या आप एक रात की दोस्ती में विश्वास रखती हैं?

Male: Maaf keejiye, kya aap ek raat ki dosti mein vishvaas rakhti hain?

माफ कीजिए, क्या आप एक रात की दोस्ती में विश्वास रखते हैं?

Female: Maaf keejiye, kya aap ek raat ki dosti mein vishvaas rakhte hain?

French
***Bonjour, je suis un étranger / une étrangère
dans cette ville, c'est où chez toi?***
*Bonjour, juh sweez un etronjay / oon etranjare
don set vee, set oo shay twah?*

Spanish
***Hola, soy nuevo / nueva en
la ciudad, ¿puedes decirme cómo se va a tu casa?***
*Oh-lah, soh-ee noo-eh-boh / noo-eh-bah ehn
la thee-oo-dahd, poo-eh-dehs deh-theer-meh koh-moh
seh bah ah too kah-sah?*

Italian
***Ciao, sono uno straniero / una straniera in questa città,
puoi indicarmi la direzione per arrivare a casa tua?***
*Chaow, so-no oo-no stra-neeay-ro / oo-na stra-neeay-ra
een kwe-sta cheet-ta, pwo-ee een-dee-kar-mee la
dee-ray-dzeeo-nay payr ar-ree-va-ray a ka-za too-a?*

German
***Hallo, ich bin fremd in dieser Stadt, kannst du mir
den Weg zu deinem Haus zeigen?***
*Hallo, ish bin fremd in deezer shtat, kanst doo meer
den veg tsu dye-nem house tseye-gen?*

Hebrew
הי, אני זר בעיר הזו, תוכלי לכוון אותי לביתך?
Hei, ani zar ba-yir ha-zo, tokhli lekhaven oti le-beitekh?

French
La seule chose qui va s'immiscer entre toi et moi, c'est une capote.
La seule shoze kee va simissay ontruh twah ay mwah, set oon capot.

✳

Spanish
Lo único que quiero que se interponga entre tú y yo es un condón.
Loh oo-nee-koh keh kee-eh-roh keh seh een-tehr-pohn-gah ehn-treh too ee yoh ehs oon kohn-dohn.

✳

Italian
L'unica cosa che deve separarci è un preservativo.
Loonee-ka ko-za ke day-vay say-parar-chee eh oo-n pray-sayr-vateevo.

✳

German
Das einzige, was ich zwischen dir und mir will, ist ein Kondom.
Das eye-ntsige, vas ish tswishen deer oond meer vil, ist ine kondom.

✳

Korean
내가 당신과 나 사이에 존재하기를
원하는 유일한 것은 콘돔입니다.
Nae-ga dang-shin-gwa na sa-i-e jon-jae-ha-gi-reul won-ha-neun yoo-il-han geut-sun condom-im-mi-da.

'Do you want to go back to my place for sex and coffee? No? You don't want coffee?'

French

**Tu veux qu'on aille chez moi pour un café et du sexe?
Non? Tu ne veux pas de café?**

*Too veuh kon eye shay mwah pour un cafay ay du sex?
Non? Too nuh veuh pa duh cafay?*

Spanish

**¿Quieres que vayamos a mi casa a hacer el amor
y tomarnos un café? ¿No? ¿No quieres un café?**

*Kee-eh-rehs keh bah-yah-mohs ah mee kah-sah ah ah-ther
ehl ah-mohr ee toh-mahr-nohs oon kah-pheh?
Noh? Noh kee-eh-rehs oon kah-pheh?*

Italian

**Vuoi venire a casa mia per un caffè
e del sesso? No? Non ti va il caffè?**

*Voo-oy vay-nee-ray a ka-za mee-a payr oo-n kaf-fe
ay dayl ses-so? No? Non tee va eel kaf-fe?*

German

**Willst du mit mir nach Hause kommen, um Kaffee zu
trinken und Sex haben? Nein? Du magst kein Kaffee?**

*Vill-st doo mit meer nack hows-eh common, oom café zoo
trinken oont sex harben? Nine? Doo magst kine-eh café?*

'Screw me if I'm wrong, but you want to sleep with me, don't you?'

French
Baise-moi si j'ai tort, mais tu veux coucher avec moi, n'est ce pas?
Baize mwah see jay tor, may too veuh cooshay avec mwah, neh se pa?

Spanish
Que me jodan si me equivoco: ¿tú quieres acostarte conmigo, no?
Keh meh hoh-dahn see meh eh-kee-boh-koh: too kee-eh-rehs ah-kohs-tahr-teh kohn-mee-goh, noh?

Italian
Fottimi se mi sbaglio, ma vuoi venire a letto con me, noh?
Fot-tee-mee say mee sba-lee-o, ma voo-oy vay-nee-ray a layt-to kon may, no?

✳

German
Ich soll verflucht sein, wenn ich mich irre, aber du willst doch mit mir schlafen, oder?
Ish sol ferflookht sine, ven ish mish eerre, aber doo vilst dokh mit meer shlafen, oder?

✳

Dutch
Ik mag doodvallen als 't niet waar is, maar je wilt met me naar bed, hè?
Ik mag dodvallun als ut neet wahr is, mahr yeuh wilt met meuh nahr bed, heh?

French

Salut, mon nom c'est Olivier, je te conseille de le retenir maintenant, parce que tu vas le crier plus tard!

Saloo, mon nom set Olivier, juh tuh consay duh luh reteneer mantuhnon, parse-kuh too va luh cre-ay ploo tar.

Spanish

Hola, me llamo Juan. Acuérdate de mi nombre, porque luego querrás gritarlo con todas tus fuerzas.

Oh-lah, mee yah-moh Hu-an Ah-koo-ehr-dah-teh deh mee nohm-breh, pohr-keh loo-eh-goh keh-rrahs gree-tahr-loh kohn toh-dahs toos phoo-ehr-thahs.

Italian

Ciao, il mio nome è Marco, ti consiglio di ricordartelo ora, perchè più tardi, lo griderai!

Chaow, eel mee-o no-may eh Mark-o, tee kon-see-lyo dee ree-kordar-taylo o-ra, payr-ke peeyoo tar-dee lo gree-day-raee!

German

Hallo, ich heiße Wilhelm. Merk ihn dir jetzt, denn später wirst du ihn sicher rausschreien.

Hallo, ish hye-seuh Vil-helm. Merk een deer jetst, den shpayter veerst doo een sisher rous-shrye-en.

French

***Que fait une gentille fille comme toi dans un esprit
mal tourné comme le mien?***

*Kuh fay une jontee fee com twah donz un espree
mal tournay com luh me-en?*

✳

Spanish

***¿Qué hace una chica tan maja como
tú en una mente tan sucia
como la mía?***

*Keh ah-theh oo-nah chee-kah tahn mah-hah koh-moh
too ehn oo-nah mehn-teh tahn soo-thee-ah
koh-moh la mee-ah?*

✳

Italian

***Che fa una ragazza perbene come te in
una mente sporca come la mia?***

*Ke fa oo-na ra-gadza payr-bay-nay ko-me tay een
oo-na mayn-te spor-ka ko-may la mee-a?*

✳

German

***Was macht ein nettes Mädchen wie du in so schmutzigen
Gedanken wie meinen?***

*Vas masht ine nettes meydshen vee doo in so shmootsigen
gedanken vee mine-en?*

✳

Danish

Hvad laver en pæn pige som dig i mine beskidte fantasier?

Va laywer en pain pee som die ee meen biskidte fantasee-a?

French
***Allons chez moi faire toutes les choses que je dirai à tout
le monde qu'on a fait de toute façon.***

*Allon shay mwah fair toot lay shoze kuh juh deeray a too
luh mond kon a fay duh toot fasson.*

Spanish
***Volvamos a mi casa a hacer lo que, de todas formas,
le contaré a todo el mundo que hemos hecho.***

*Bohl-bah-mohs ah mee kah-sah ah ah-ther loh keh deh
toh-dahs fohr-mahs leh kohn-tah-reh ah toh-doh ehl
moon-doh khe eh-mohs eh-choh.*

Italian
***Andiamo da me a fare tutte le cose che ad ogni
modo dirò a tutti abbiamo fatto.***

*An-deea-mo da may a faa-ray toot-tay lay ko-ze ke ad ony
mo-do dee-ro a toot-tee ab-beeamo fat-to.*

German
***Komm mit zu mir und lass uns all die Dinge tun,
von denen ich hinterher ohnehin behaupten werde,
dass wir sie gemacht haben.***

*Kom meet tsu meer oond las oons al dee din-geuh toon,
von denen ish hinterher ohneheen behoupten ver-deuh,
das veer zee gemasht ha-ben.*

> **'I like maths. How about we go to my room, add the bed, subtract your clothes, divide your legs and multiply?'**

French

J'aime les maths. Si on allait dans ma chambre, qu'on ajoutait le lit, soustrayait tes fringues, divisait tes jambes et qu'on se multipliait?

Jame lay math. See on allay don ma shombruh, kon ajoutay luh lee, soostray-ay tay frang, divizay tay jombe ay kon suh multiple-ay?

Spanish

Me gustan las matemáticas. ¿Qué te parece si vamos a mi habitación, sumamos la cama, restamos la ropa, dividimos tus piernas y nos multiplicamos?

Meh goos-tahn lahs mah-teh-mah-tee-kahs. Keh teh pah-reh-theh see bah-mohs ah mee ah-bee-tah-thee-ohn, soo-mah-mohs la kah-mah, rehs-tah-mohs la roh-pah, dee-bee-dee-mohs toos pee-ehr-nahs ee nohs mool-tee-plee-kah-mohs?

∗

Italian

Mi piace la matematica. Che ne diresti di andare in camera mia ad eseguire la somma del letto, la sottrazione dei tuoi vestiti, la divisione delle tue gambe e la nostra moltiplicazione?

Mee peea-che la matay-matee-ka. Ke nay dee-raystee dee an-daray een ka-mayra mee-a ad e-saygooee-ray la som-ma dayl layt-to, la sot-tratseeonay day too-oy vay-stee-tee, la deevee-seeonay dayl-lay too-ay gam-bay ay la no-stra moltee-pleeka-tseeonay?

German

Ich mag Mathe. Wie wäre es, wenn du mit zu mir kommst und wir das Bett addieren, deine Kleidungsstücke abziehen, deine Beine teilen und dann mehrmals kommen?

Ish mag mat-te. Vee vay-reuh es, ven doo mit tsu meer komst oond veer das bet adeeren, dye-neuh klye-doongs-shtoocke abtseehen, dye-neuh bine-euh tye-len oond dan mermals komen?

Czech

Jsem na matematiku. Co kdybychom šli do mého pokoje, přičetli postel, odečetli tvoje oblečení, rozdělili ti nohy a znásobili se?

Ysem na matematikoo. Tso kdibikhom shli do meho pokoye, przhichetli postel, odechetli tvoye oblechenyee, rozdyelili tyi nohi a znaasobili seh?

Global Sex Facts

One in ten people think Brazilians are the sexiest people on earth followed by Americans and the French.

According to the 2005 Durex Global Sex Survey, globally people have had an average number of nine sexual partners. According to the same survey, Turks have had more partners than any other country (14.5) and Indians the least (3).

French
J'ai un préservatif qui porte ton nom.
Jay un prezurvateef kee port ton nom.

Spanish
Tengo un condón que lleva escrito tu nombre.
Tehn-goh oon kohn-dohn keh yeh-bah ehs-krih-toh too nohm-breh.

Italian
Ho un preservativo col tuo nome scritto sopra.
Oh oo-n praysayr-vateevo kol too-o no-may screet-to so-pra.

German
Ich habe ein Kondom mit deinem Namen d'rauf.
Ish ha-beuh ine kondom mit dye-nem nahmen drouf.

Russian
У меня презервати́в с твои́м и́менем на нём.
Oo minya prizirvativ s tvaim imenem na niom.

Global Sex Fact

According to a recent survey, 44 per cent of adults worldwide have had a one-night stand, with 22 per cent claiming to have had an extra-marital affair.

French
***Salut, je suis l'amour de ta vie. On m'a dit
que tu me cherchais?***
*Saloo, juh swee l'amoor duh ta vee. On ma dee
kuh too muh shershay?*

✳

Spanish
***Hola, soy el amor de tu vida. Me han
dicho que me buscabas.***
*Oh-lah, soh-ee ehl ah-mohr deh too bee-dah. Meh ahn
dee-choh keh meh boos-kah-bahs.*

✳

Italian
***Ciao, sono il tuo uomo ideale. Qualcuno mi
ha detto che mi stavi cercando?***
*Chaow, so-no eel too-o wo-mo eedayah-lee. Kwal-koono mee
a dayt-to ke mee sta-vee cher-kando?*

✳

German
***Hallo, ich bin der Richtige. Jemand sagte,
dass du mir suchst?***
*Hallo, ish bin dare rishtig-eh. Yay-mand saag-teh
dass doo meer zook-st?*

✳

Hindi
हैलो, मेरा नाम प्यारे है। किसी ने बताया कि आप मुझे ढूंढ रही थीं?
*Hello, main toomhaare sapanon kaa raajkoomar hoon . . .
Kisi ne bataaya ki aap moojhe dhoond rahi theen?*

'Do you believe in love at first sight, or should I walk by again?'

French
Tu crois aux coups de foudre, ou tu veux que je repasse?
Too crwah o coo duh foodruh, oo too veuh kuh juh ruhpass?

Spanish
***¿Crees en el amor a primera vista,
o tengo que pasearme otra vez
por delante de ti?***
*Kreh-ehs ehn ehl ah-mohr ah pree-meh-rah bees-tah,
oh tehn-goh keh pah-seh-ahr-meh oh-trah behth
pohr deh-lahn-teh deh tee?*

Italian
***Credi nell'amore a prima vista, o devo
ripassare?***
*Kre-dee nayl-lamo-ray a pree-ma vee-sta, or day-vo
ree-pas-saray?*

German
***Glaubst du an Liebe auf den ersten Blick, oder soll
ich noch einmal vorbeilaufen?***
*Gloubst doo an lee-beuh ouf den ersten blick, oder sol
ish nokh ine-mal forbye-loufen?*

Hebrew
את מאמינה באהבה ממבט ראשון, או שאצטרך
לעבור כאן שוב?
*At maamina be-ahava mi-mabat rishon, o she-etztarekh
la'avor can shuv?*

French

**Si je te disais que tu as un beau corps,
tu m'en tiendrais rigueur?**

*See juh tuh deezay kuh too a un boh corps,
too mon te-endray rigeur?*

✳

Spanish

**Si te digo que tienes un cuerpo precioso,
¿me lo restregarás por la cara?**

*See teh dee-goh keh tee-eh-nehs oon koo-ehr-poh preh-thee-
oh-soh, meh loh rrehs-treh-gah-rahs pohr la kah-rah?*

✳

Italian

**Se ti dicessi che hai un bel corpo,
lo stringeresti sul mio?**

*Say tee dee-ches-see ke aee oo-n bayl kor-po,
lo streenjay-raystee sool mee-o?*

✳

German

**Wenn ich sage, dass du einen tollen Körper hast,
würdest du es mich spüren lassen?**

*Ven ish sa-geuh, das doo eye-nen tollen keurper hast,
voordest doo es mish shpooren lassen?*

✳

Thai

ถ้าฉันบอกว่าคุณมีรูปร่างที่สมส่วน คุณจะแย้งฉันไหม

*Taa chan bok wa khoon mii roobrang tii som suan khoon
ja yeng chán mai?*

French
A part être sexy, tu fais quoi dans la vie?
A par etruh sexy, too fay kwah don la vee?

Spanish
Aparte de a ser sexy, ¿a qué te dedicas?
Ah-pahr-teh deh ah sehr seh-xee ah keh teh deh-dee-kahs?

Italian
Oltre ad essere sexy, che lavoro fai?
Ol-tray ad essay-ray sexy, ke la-voro fa-ee?

German
Außer sexy auszusehen, was machst du sonst noch?
Ousser sexy ous-tsoo-sehen, vas mashst doo sonst nokh?

Dutch
Wat doe je voor de kost, behalve sexy zijn?
Waht doo yeuh vor deuh cost, beuhalveuh sexy zeyn?

Travellers' Tip

If you're a red-blooded male looking for a good time, head down under. Surveys suggest that Australian women have sex on the first date more than women the same age in the USA and Canada.

'Let me show you the way to heaven.'

French
Laisse-moi te montrer la voie du paradis.
Lace mwah tuh montray la vwoi doo paradee.

*

Spanish
**Déjame que te muestre el camino
del cielo.**
*Deh-hah-meh keh teh moo-ehs-treh ehl kah-mee-noh
dehl thee-eh-loh.*

*

Italian
Lasciami mostrarti la via del paradiso.
Lasheea-mee mo-strar-tee la vee-a dayl para-deeso.

*

German
Komm, ich zeig dir den Weg in den Himmel.
Kom, ish tseye-g deer den veg in den himmel.

*

Danish
Lad mig vise dig vejen til paradis.
La my vees da vie-en te paradees.

Global Sex Fact

*The gallbladder of the black bear is one
of the most sought-after aphrodisiacs
in the Far East.*

French
Toi. Moi. Crème chantilly. Menottes. Des questions?
Twah. Mwah. Crem shont-ee-ee. Menott. Day kesteeon?

∗

Spanish
Tú. Yo. Mucha nata. Esposas.
¿Alguna pregunta?
Too. Yoh. Moo-chah nah-tah. Ehs-poh-sahs.
Ahl-goo-nah preh-goon-tah?

∗

Italian
Te. Me. Panna montata. Manette.
Hai qualche domanda?
Tay. May. Pan-na mon-tata. Ma-nayt-te.
Aee kwal-ke do-man-da?

∗

German
Du. Mich. Schlagsahne. Eine Schele.
Hast du fragen?
Doo. Mish. Shlarg-sarn-euh. Ine-euh shay-ler.
Hass-t doo fraagen?

∗

Finnish
Sä ja mä. Kermavaahtoa ja käsiraudat.
Onko kysymyksiä?
Say ya ma. Kermavakhtoya kasiraudat.
Onko koosoomooksiya?

'I lost my puppy. Can you help me find him? I think he went to this cheap hotel room.'

French

***J'ai perdu mon chiot. Tu peux m'aider à le retrouver?
Je crois qu'il est allé dans cette chambre d'hôtel miteux.***

*Jay pairdoo mon sheot. Too peuh mayday a luh retroovay?
Je crwah kill et allay don set shombruh dotel meeteuh.*

Spanish

***He perdido mi cachorrito. ¿Me ayudas a buscarlo? Creo que
se ha metido en una habitación de ese hotel.***

*Eh pehr-dee-doh mee kah-cho-rrih-toh. Meh ah-yoo-dahs ah
boos-kahr-loh? Kreh-oh keh seh ah meh-tee-doh ehn oo-nah
ah-bee-tah-thee-ohn deh eh-seh oh-tehl.*

Italian

***Ho perso il mio cagnolino. Puoi aiutarmi a ritrovarlo? Credo
che sia andato in questa conveniente camera
di albergo.***

*Oh payr-so eel mee-o kanyo-leeno. Pwo-ee a-yootar-mee
a reetro-varlo? Kre-do ke see-a an-dato een kwe-sta
con-vayneeayn-tay ka-mayra dee al-bayrgo.*

German

***Ich habe meinen Hund verloren. Kannst du mir helfen, ihn zu
finden? Ich glaube, er ist in dieses billige
Hotelzimmer gegangen.***

*Ish ha-beuh mye-nen hoond ferloren. Kanst doo meer helfen,
een tsu finden? Ish gloube, er ist in deeses billige
hoteltsimer gegangen.*

French
Quelle belle paire de jambes.
A quelle heure s'ouvrent-elles?
Kell bell pair duh jomb. A kell eur soovret-ell?

✳

Spanish
Vaya par de piernas. ¿A qué hora abren?
Bah-yah pahr deh pee-ehrr-nahs. Ah keh oh-rah ah-brehn?

✳

Italian
Che bel paio di gambe. A che ora aprono?
Kay bayl pa-yo dee gam-bay. A ke o-ra a-prono?

✳

German
Das sind hübsche Beine – und wann öffnen sie?
Das sind hoobshe bine-euh – oond van euffnen see?

✳

Russian
Хоро́шенькие но́жки, а когда́ они́ открыва́ются?
Haroshenikie nozhki, a kagda ani atkryvayootsya?

Global Sex Fact

Up until the second century BC
it was considered common practice for
older Greek men to indulge in pederasty
or homosexual relationships with youths.

French
Salut, je m'appelle . . . mais tu peux m'appeler 'Sexy Boy'.
Saloo, juh mapell . . . may too peuh mapellay 'Sexy Boy'.

✳

Spanish
Hola, me llamo . . . pero puedes llamarme 'amante'.
Oh-lah, meh yah-moh . . . peh-roh poo-eh-dehs yah-mah-meh 'am-ant-eh'.

✳

Italian
Salve, mi chiamo . . . ma tu puoi chiamarmi 'amante'.
Sal-ve, mee keea-mo . . . ma too pwo-ee keea-marmee 'aman-tay'.

✳

German
Hallo, ich heiße . . . aber du kanns mich 'Liebhaber' nennen.
Hallo, ish hy-seuh . . . arber doo can-st mish leeb-harber nennen.

✳

Thai
สวัสดี ฉันชื่อ...แต่คุณเรียกฉันว่า'ที่รัก'ได้
Sawaddii chan cheu . . . dae khoon riak chan wa tii rak dai.

'You must be tired because you've been running through my mind all day.'

French

Tu dois être fatigué / fatiguée parce que tu as trotté dans ma tête toute la journée.

Too dwoi etruh fatigay parse-kuh too a trottay don ma tet toot la journay.

Spanish

Seguro que te resulta agotador estar rondándome la cabeza todo el día.

Seh-goo-roh keh teh rreh-sool-tah ah-goh-tah-dohr ehs-tahr rrohn-dahn-doh-meh la kah-beh-thah toh-doh ehl dee-ah.

Italian

Devi essere stanco / stanca visto che hai attraversato tutto il giorno nella mia mente.

Day-vee es-say-ray stan-ko / stan-ka vee-sto ke aee at-travayrsa-to toot-to eel joe-rno nayl-la mee-a mayn-tay.

Travellers' Tip

It would seem that sun and sex really do go hand in hand. When picking a season to go abroad, ladies should bear in mind that men's testosterone levels are highest in the summer.

German

**_Du musst müde sein, schließlich bist du den ganzen
Tag durch meine Gedanken gejagt._**

*Doo moost moode sine, shleeslish bist doo den gantsen
taag doorsh mye-neuh gedanken geyaagt.*

✳

Hindi

आप ज़रूर थक गयी होंगी क्योंकि आज पूरा दिन आप मेरे दिमाग में घूमती
रहीं ।

*Male: Aap zaroor thuk gayee hongi kyonki aaj poora din aap
mere dimag mein ghoomti rahin.*

आप ज़रूर थक गयी होंगे क्योंकि आज पूरा दिन आप मेरे दिमाग में घूमते
रहे ।

*Female: Aap zaroor thuk gaye honge kyonki aaj poora din
aap mere dimag mein ghoomte rahe.*

Global Sex Fact

*A 21.94-metre condom was fitted over the
obelisk in the Place de la Concorde, Paris,
France, on December 1, 1993, to mark
the annual World AIDS day. The giant
latex creation was funded by the Italian
clothes firm Benetton.*

'Was your father a thief? Because someone stole the stars from the sky and put them in your eyes.'

French
Ton père était-il un voleur? Parce que quelqu'un a piqué les étoiles du ciel et les a mises dans tes yeux.
Ton pare et-ait il un voleur? Pars-kuh kelkun a peekay lez etwahle doo se-el ay lez a mize don tez yeuh.

Spanish
¿Tu padre era ladrón? Porque alguien ha robado todas las estrellas del cielo y las ha puesto en tus ojos.
Too pah-dreh eh-rah lah-drohn? Pohr-keh ahl-ghee-ehn ah roh-bah-doh toh-dahs lahs ehs-treh-yahs dehl thee-eh-loh ee lahs ah poo-ehs-toh ehn toos oh-hohs.

Italian
Tuo padre era un ladro? Perchè qualcuno ha rubato le stelle dal cielo e le ha messe nei tuoi occhi.
Too-o pa-dray e-ra oo-n la-dro? Payr-ke kwal-koono a rooba-to lay stayl-lay dal cheeay-lo ay lay a mays-say nay too-oee ok-ee.

German
War dein Vater ein Dieb? Da jemand die Sterne vom Himmel gestohlen hat, und sie in deine Augen gesetzt hat.
Var dye-n farter eye-n deeb? Dar yay-mand dee shter-neuh fomm himmel geshtoe-len hat und zee in dye-neuh owgen gesetst hat.

French

J'ai perdu ma virginité. Je peux avoir la tienne?

Jay pairdoo ma verjinitay. Juh puh avwoir la te-en?

✳

Spanish

He perdido la virginidad.
¿Me das la tuya?

Eh pehr-dee-doh mee beer-hee-nee-dahd
meh dahs la too-yah.

✳

Italian

Io ho perso la mia verginità,
posso avere la tua?

Ee-o oh payr-so la mee-a ver-jeeneeta,
pos-so avay-ray la too-a?

✳

German

Ich habe meine Unschuld verloren.
Kann ich deine haben?

Ish ha-beuh mye-neh oonshoolt ferlore-ren.
Can ish dye-neh harben?

✳

Danish

Jeg har mistet min mødom. Må jeg tage din?

Ya ha mistet meen merdom. Maw ya tay deen?

'I'll make you so hot you'll come away with a tan!'

French
Je vais tellement te chauffer que tu vas repartir bronze / bronzée!
Juh vay telmon tuh showfay kuh too va repartear bronzay!

Spanish
Te pondré tan caliente que acabarás morena.
Teh poh-dreh tahn kah-lee-ehn-teh keh ah-kah-bah-rahs moh-reh-nah.

Italian
Ti infiammerò così tanto da farti abbronzare!
Tee eenfeeam-mayro ko-si tan-to da far-tee ab-bron-zaray!

*

German
Ich mach dich so heiß, dass du aufpassen musst, keinen Sonnenbrand zu bekommen!
Ish mash dish zo hyse, das doo ouf-passen moost, kine-en sonenbrand tsoo bekomen!

Global Sex Fact

The ancient Greek historian Herodotus claimed that the marriage traditions of the Nasamones of Libya required the bride to have sex with all the males in attendance at the wedding party.

French

Allez ma belle, laisse-moi te transpercer avec mon épée d'amour.

Allay ma bell, lace mwah tuh tronspersay avec mon epay damour.

✳

Spanish

Venga a mí, señora, y permítame que la ensarte con mi espada de amor.

Behn-gah ah mee, seh-nee-oh-rah, ee pehr-mee-tah-meh keh la ehn-sahr-teh kohn mee ehs-pah-dah deh ah-mohr.

✳

Italian

Vieni qui da me e lasciami trafiggerti con la mia spada d'amore.

Veeay-nee kwee da may ay la-sheeamee trafi-jayrtee kon la mee-a spa-da amo-ray.

✳

German

Komm zu mir, edles Fräulein, und lass dich von meinem Schwert der Liebe erlegen.

Kom tsu meer, edles froi-line, oond las dish fon mye-nem shvert der lee-beuh erlegen.

✳

Czech

Pojd' ke mně, má dámo, a dovol mi, abych tě sťal svým mečem lásky.

Poyd ke mnye, maa daamo, a dovol mi abykh tye styal sveem mechem laasky.

'Congratulations, you've just won the keys to the city and I'm your guide.'

French
Félicitations, tu viens juste de gagner les clés de la ville et moi, je suis ton guide.
Felisetasseon, too ve-en joost duh ganyay lay clay duh la vee ay mwah, juh swee ton geed.

✳

Spanish
Enhorabuena, acabas de ganar las llaves de la ciudad y yo soy tu guía.
Ehn-oh-rah-boo-eh-nah, ah-kah-bahs deh gah-nahr lahs yah-behs deh la thee-oo-dahd ee yoh soh-ee too gee-ah.

✳

Italian
Congratulazioni, hai appena vinto le chiavi della città e io sono la tua guida.
Kon-gratoola-tseeonee, aee ap-payna veen-to lay keea-vee dayl-la chet-ta ay ee-o so-no la too-a gooee-da.

✳

German
Herzlichen Glückwunsch! Du hast soeben den Schlüssel zur Stadt gewonnen, und ich bin dein Führer.
Herts-lishen gloockvoonsh! Doo hast so-eben den shloosel tsoor shtat gevonnen, oond ish bin dine foohrer.

✳

Russian
Поздравляю,
Вы то́лько что вы́играли ключи́ от го́рода, и я – Ваш гид.
Pazdravliayoo, vy toliko shto vyigrali klioochi aht gorada, ee ya – vash gheed.

French
***J'ai perdu mon numéro de téléphone,
tu peux me prêter le tien?***
*Jay pairdoo mon numero duh telephone,
too peuh muh pretay luh te-en?*

✳

Spanish
***He perdido mi número de teléfono.
¿Me das el tuyo?***
*Eh pehr-dee-doh mee noo-meh-roh deh teh-leh-foh-noh.
Meh dahs ehl too-yoh?*

✳

Italian
***Ho perso il mio numero di telefono,
potrei avere in prestito il tuo?***
*Oh payr-so eel mee-o noo-mayro dee tay-layfono,
po-tray avay-ray een praystee-to eel too-o?*

✳

German
***Ich habe meine Telefonnummer verloren,
kann ich mir deine ausborgen?***
*Ish ha-beuh mye-neuh telefon-numer ferloren,
kan ish meer dye-neuh ousborgen?*

✳

Portuguese
***Eu perdi o meu numero de telefone,
você pode prestâ-me o seu?***
*Ay-oo pehr-dee oh meh-ooh noo-mehr-oh dee tel-eh-foh-nee,
vos-eh poh-dee prest-ar-meh oh seh-oo?*

French
Plus la peine de chercher, me voilà.
Ploo la pen duh shurshay, muh vwoila.

Spanish
Tu búsqueda ha terminado. Aquí estoy.
Too boos-keh-dah ah tehr-mee-nah-doh ah-kee ehs-toh-ee.

Italian
La tua ricerca è terminata, eccomi.
La too-a ree-cherka e tayr-meenata, eko-mee.

✲

German
Deine Suche ist zu Ende. Hier bin ich.
Dye-neh zoo-ker ist zoo ender. Here bin ish.

✲

Hindi
आप की तलाश पूरी हो गई, मैं आ गया हूं।
Male: Aapki talaash poori ho gayee. Maen aa gayaa hoon.

आप की तलाश पूरी हो गई, मैं आ गई हूं।
Female: Aapki talaash poori ho gayee. Maen aa gayee hoon.

Global Sex Fact

*Males of the island of Tikopia are forbidden
to touch any genitals, including their own.*

French
**Mon ami / amie là-bas veut savoir si tu penses
que je suis mignon / mignonne.**
Mon amee laba veuh savwoir see too ponce
kuh juh swee minyon / minyonne.

✳

Spanish
**Mi amigo / amiga quiere saber si
crees que soy guapo / guapa.**
Mee ah-mee-goh / ah-mee-gah kee-eh-reh sah-behr see
kreh-ehs keh soh-ee woo-ha-poh / woo-ha-pah.

✳

Italian
**Il mio amico / La mia amica laggiù vuole
sapere se pensi che io sia carino / carina.**
Eel mee-o amee-ko / La mee-a amee-ka la-jyou voo-olay
sa-payray say payn-see ke ee-o see-a ka-reeno / ka-reena.

✳

German
Mein Freund will wissen, ob du mich schön findest.
Mine froy-nd vill vissen ob doo mish shern findest.

✳

Swedish
Min kompis där borta vill veta ifall du tycker jag är söt.
Min kompis dar borta vill ve-eta ifall dui tooker yaag ar soet.

✳

Hebrew
חמוד.חברי שיושב שם רוצה לדעת אם את חושבת שאני
Khaveri she-yoshev sham rotse ladaat im at khoshevet
she-ani khamood.

> **'Of all the chairs, in all the bars, in all the world,**
> **and you have to sit next to mine.'**

French

***De toutes les chaises, dans tous les bars, dans le monde
entier, tu devais t'asseoir dans celle à côté de la mienne.***

*De toot lay shaze, don too lay bar, don luh mond
ont-e-ay, too devay tasswoir don sell a coatay duh la me-en.*

Spanish

***Con todas las sillas de todos los bares
del mundo, y has tenido que sentarte a mi lado.***

*Kohn toh-dahs lahs see-yahs deh toh-dohs lohs bah-rehs
dehl moon-doh, ee ahs teh-nee-doh keh sehn-tahr-teh
ah mee lah-doh.*

Italian

***Di tutte le sedie, in tutti i bar, in tutto
il mondo sei venuto/a a sederti vicino a me.***

*Dee toot-tay lay say-deeay, een toot-tee ee bar, een toot-to
eel mon-do say vay-nooto/a a say-dayrtee vee-cheeno a may.*

German

***Von allen Sitzen in allen Bars auf der ganzen Welt musst
du ausgerechnet neben mir sitzen.***

*Fon allen sitsen in allen bars ouf der gantsen velt moost
doo ousgereshnet neben meer sitsen.*

Thai

มีเก้าอี้ตั้งมากมายไม่ว่าบาร์ไหนที่ใดใน โลก คุณจะต้องนั่งข้างฉัน

*Mii gao-ii dang maak mai, mai wa bar nai, tii dai nai lok,
khoon ja dong nang khang chan.*

'Why don't you come over here, sit on my lap and we'll talk about the first thing that pops up?'

French
Viens t'asseoir sur mes genoux et nous parlerons de la première chose qui surgit.
Ve-en tasswoir sur may jenoo ay noo parleron duh la prem-e-air shoze kee surjee.

Spanish
¿Por qué no vienes aquí, te sientas en mi regazo y hablamos de la primera cosa que salga?
Pohr keh noh bee-eh-nehs ah-kee teh see-ehn-tahs ehn mee rreh-gah-thoh ee ah-blah-mohs deh la pree-meh-rah koh-sah keh sahl-gah?

Italian
Perchè non vieni a séderti sul mio grembo e parliamo della prima cosa che spunta?
Payr-ke non veeay-nee a saydayr-tee sool mee-o graym-bo ay par-leeamo dayl-la pree-ma ko-za ke spoon-ta?

German
Warum kommst du nicht rüber, setzt dich auf meinen Schoß und wir sprechen über das Erste, was hochkommt?
Varoom komst doo nisht roober, setst dish ouf mye-nen shoss oond veer shpreshen oober das erste, vas hokh-kommt?

French
**Quelle belle robe. Je la vois bien par terre
dans ma chambre.**
Kell bell robe. Juh la vwoih be-en par tare
don ma shombruh.

Spanish
**Llevas un vestido muy bonito.
Quedaría precioso en el suelo
de mi habitación.**
Yeh-bahs oon behs-tee-doh moo-ee boh-nee-toh.
Keh-dah-ree-ah preh-thee-oh-soh ehn ehl soo-eh-loh
deh mee ah-bee-tah-thee-ohn.

Italian
**Che bel vestito. Andrebbe molto bene sul
pavimento della mia camera da letto.**
Ke bayl vaystee-to. An-drayb-bay mol-to bay-nay sool
pa-veemayn-to dayl-la mee-a ka-mayra da layt-to.

Essential Vocabulary

To spank, *verb*

French ***fesser***
Spanish ***pegarle***
Italian ***sculacciare***
German ***schlagen, spanken***

German

Das ist ein schönes Kleid. Es würde auf dem Boden meines Zimmers besonders gut aussehen.

Das ist ine scherness klite. Ess verdeuh ouf dame boh-den mye-nes tsimmers berzonders goot ouszayen.

✳

Swedish

Vilken fin klänning. Den skulle se jätte bra ut pa golvet i mitt sovrum.

Vikken feen klenning. Den skolle sie yette bra ut puo golvet ee mitt suovrom.

✳

Welsh

Dyna frog bert, fasa fo yn edrych yn well ar llawr fy ystafell wely.

Dinna frog bairt, va-sa vor en edrich en wesh ar clower ver estarvesh welly.

✳

Korean

드레스가 멋있군요. 내 침실 바닥과 잘 어울려요.

Dress-ga meut-sit-goon yo. Nae chim-sil ba-dag-gwa jal eu-ool-lyeu-yo.

Global Sex Fact

Every day, 200 million couples around the world have sex, which is about 2000 couples at any given moment.

'Here's 50p, phone your mum up and tell her you won't be coming home.'

French

***Tiens, voilà 1 Euro, appelle ta mère et dis lui
que tu ne rentres pas ce soir.***

*Te-en, vwoila un Euro, appell ta mare ay dee lui
kuh too nuh rontruh paz suh swoir.*

Spanish

***Aquí tienes 1 Euro, llama a tu
madre y dile que no volverás a casa.***

*Ah-kee tee-eh-nehs oon eh-oo-roh, yah-mah ah too
mah-dreh ee dee-leh keh noh bohl-beh-rahs ah kah-sah.*

Italian

***Tieni, ecco 1 Euro, chiama tua madre
e dille che non torni a casa questa sera.***

*Teeay-nee, e-ko oo-n ayoo-ro, keea-ma too-a ma-dray
ay deel-lay ke non tor-nee a ka-za kwe-sta say-ra.*

German

***Hier sind 1 Euro. Ruf deine Mutter an und sag ihr,
dass du heute nicht nach Hause kommst.***

*Heer sind ein oiro. Roof dye-neuh mooter an oond zag eer,
dass doo hoi-teuh nisht nakh house-euh komst.*

Danish

***Her har du 2 kroner, så du kan ringe og sige,
at du ikke kommer hjem og sover.***

*Her har doo tow kroner, so doo kan reng o see,
a doo kommer yem o sower.*

French
Je t'invite à dîner si tu me prépares le petit dej.
Juh tanveet a dinay see too muh prepar luh petee dej.

✻

Spanish
**Te invito a cenar si tú me haces
el desayuno.**
Teh een-bee-toh ah theh-nahr see too meh ah-thehs
ehl dehs-ah-yoo-noh.

✻

Italian
Ti invito a cena, se mi prepari la colazione.
Tee een-veeto a che-na, say mee pray-paree la
ko-latseeo-nay.

✻

German
**Ich lade dich zum Abendessen ein,
wenn du mir das Frühstuck kochst.**
Ish larder dish zoom arbend-essen ine,
venn doo meer das froo-shtook kockst.

✻

Czech
Pozvu tě na večeři, když mě pozveš na snídani.
Pozvoo tye na vecherzhi, kdyzh mnye pozvesh na sneedanyi.

✻

Portuguese
**Eu compro você o jantar se você me compra
café-da-amanhã.**
Ay-oo comp-roh vos-eh oh jant-ah seh vos-eh me comp-rah
caf-eh-dah-man-yah.

Date

French
Une table pour deux, s'il vous plaît.
Oon tabbluh pour deuh, sil voo play.

✳

Spanish
Mesa para dos, por favor.
Meh-sah pah-rah dohs, pohr fah-bohr.

✳

Italian
Un tavolo per due, per favore.
Oo-n tavo-lo payr doo-ay, payr fa-voray.

✳

German
Ein Tisch für zwei Personen, bitte.
Ine tish fyour ts-vie per-zone-en, bitter.

✳

Swedish
Bord för tva, tack.
Boord for tvuo, tack.

✳

Welsh
Bwrdd i ddau, plîs.
Borth ee thiy, plees.

'Your place or mine?'

French

On va chez toi ou chez moi?

On va shay twah ou shay mwah?

✻

Spanish

¿En tu casa o en la mía?

Ehn too kah-sah oh ehn la mee-ah?

✻

Italian

A casa tua o a casa mia?

A ka-za too-a o a ka-za mee-a?

✻

German

Bei dir zu Hause oder bei mir?

By deer tsoo howser oder by meer?

✻

Portuguese

A sua casa o na minha?

A soo-ah cah-sah oh na meen-yah?

Travellers' Tip

If you're a fan of sex toys, head down under or stateside. Sex using vibrators is most commonly practised in Australia and the USA.

French
Tu veux rentrer prendre un café?
Too veuh rontray prondruh un cafay?

✳

Spanish
¿Quieres subir a tomarte un café?
Kee-eh-rehs soo-beer ah toh-mahr-teh oon kah-pheh?

✳

Italian
Vuoi venire a prenderti un caffè?
Voo-oee vay-neeray a prayn-dayrtee oo-n kaf-fe?

✳

German
Willst du auf einen Kaffee mit reinkommen?
Veelst doo ouf ine-en cafe mit rine-komen?

✳

Hindi
कॉफी के लिए अंदर आओगी?
Male: Coffee ke liye under aanaa chaahogi?

कॉफी के लिए अंदर आओगे?
Female: Coffee ke liye under aanaa chaahoge?

Global Sex Fact

*Worldwide, women's top choice of partners
are Italians and the Spanish, while men
go for the Chinese and Brazilians.*

French
Tu veux voir ma collection de timbres?
Too veuh vwoir ma collec-se-on duh tambruh

✳

Spanish
¿Quieres ver mi colección de sellos?
Kee-eh-rehs behr mee koh-lehk-thee-ohn deh seh-yohs?

✳

Italian
**Ti piacerebbe vedere la mia collezione
di francobolli?**
*Tee peeache-rayb-bay vay-dayray la mee-a kol-laytseeo-nay
dee fran-kobol-lee?*

✳

German
Soll ich dir meine Briefmarkensammlung zeigen?
Sol ish deer mye-neuh breefmarkensamloong tsye-gen?

✳

Hebrew
רוצה לראות את אוסף הבולים שלי?
Rotsa lirot et osef ha-bulim sheli?

Global Sex Fact

*The origin of the word 'orgasm' is from
the ancient Greek orgaein, meaning
'to swell' or 'to be excited or lustful'.*

French

**Attends-moi ici, je vais descendre ma collection
d'estampes japonaises.**

Atton mwah eesee, juh vay desondruh ma collec-se-on
destomp japonez.

✳

Spanish

**Espérate aquí, que te enseñaré
mi colección de sellos.**

Ehs-peh-rah-teh ah-kee, keh teh ehn-seh-nee-ah-reh
mee koh-lehk-thee-ohn deh seh-yohs.

✳

Italian

Aspetta qui, vado a prendere le incisioni.

Aspayt-ta kwi, va-do a prayn-dayray lay een-cheeseeo-nee.

✳

German

**Warte mal hier, ich hole meine
Kupferstiche runter.**

Var-te mal heer, ish ho-leuh mye-neuh
koopfer-shtishe roonter.

✳

Korean

여기서 기다리세요, 그 에칭작품을 갖고
내려 올께요

Yeu-gi-seu gi-da-ri-se-yo, geu e-ching-jak-poom-eul
gat-go nae-ryeu ol-kae-yo.

Foreplay

French
Bien sûr que j'ai apporté des capotes!
Be-en soor kuh jay aportay day capot!

✳

Spanish
¡Pues claro que he traído condones!
Poo-ehs klah-roh keh eh trah-ee-doh kohn-doh-nehs!

✳

Italian
Certo che ho portato dei preservativi!
Cher-to ke oh por-tato ee pray-sayrvatee-vee!

✳

German
Natürlich habe ich Kondome mitgebracht!
Natoorlish ha-beuh ish condomer mitgeuhbrackt!

✳

Portuguese
Claro que tenho camisinhas!
Clahro que tainyu camizeenyas!

✳

Swedish
Det är klart att jag har kondomer med mig!
Diet aer klart att yaag haar mied conduome!

✳

Welsh
Wrth gwrs fod gennyf sachau dyrnu!
Orth gors vod gennev sachai durny!

French
Je te montre le mien si tu me montres le tien.
Juh tuh montruh luh me-en se too muh montruh luh te-en.

✳

Spanish
**Yo te enseño lo mío
si tú me enseñas lo tuyo.**
*Yoh teh ehn-seh-nee-oh loh mee-oh
see too meh ehn-seh-nee-ahs loh too-yoh.*

✳

Italian
Ti mostro il mio, se tu mi mostri la tua.
Tee mo-stro eel mee-o, say too mee mo-stree la too-a.

✳

German
**Ich zeige dir meine,
wenn du mir deine zeigst.**
*Ish tsye-geuh deer mye-neuh,
ven doo meer dye-neuh tsyegst.*

✳

Thai
ฉันจะโชว์ของฉันให้ดู ถ้าคุณโชว์ของคุณ
Chan ja show kong chan hai doo, ta khoon show kong khoon.

French
Mon dieu, elle est énorme!
Mon dyeu, elle et enorme!

✳

Spanish
¡Dios mío, es enorme!
Dee-ohs mee-oh, ehs eh-nohr-meh!

✳

Italian
Caspita, è enorme!
Ka-speeta e e-normay!

✳

German
Mann, es ist riesig!
Man, ess ist reezig!

✳

Danish
Wow – den er stor!
Wow – den er stor!

Global Sex Fact

*The term 'missionary position' originates
from the time when Oceanic people were
urged by missionaries to adopt the 'man
on top' position as it was considered
the only morally acceptable way
to have intercourse.*

French
Tais-toi et embrasse-moi.
Tay twah ay ombrass mwah.

∗

Spanish
Cállate y bésame.
Kah-yah-teh ee beh-sah-meh.

∗

Italian
Stai zitto / zitta e baciami.
Sta-ee dzeet-to / dzee-ta ay bacheea-mee.

∗

German
Sei still und küss mich.
Z-eye shtill oond kooss mish.

∗

Dutch
Hou je mond en kus me.
How yeuh mond en kus mooh.

Essential Vocabulary

To kiss, *verb*

French **embrasser**
Spanish **besar**
Italian **baciare**
German **küssen**
Swedish **kyssa**

French
Tu veux que je te fasse un strip-tease?
Too veuh kuh juh tuh fass un strip-tease?

*

Spanish
¿Quieres que te haga un estriptís?
Kee-eh-rehs keh teh ah-gah oon ehs-treep-tees?

*

Italian
Desideri che ti faccia un ballo erotico?
Daysee-dayree ke tee fa-cheea oo-n bal-lo ero-teeko?

*

German
Soll ich für dich einen Laptanz aufführen?
Sol ish foor dish eye-nen laptants ouf-foohren?

*

Danish
Vil du have solostrip?
Vil doo hey solostrip?

Global Sex Fact

*The word 'fornication' derives from
the Latin word* **fornix,** *meaning 'archway',
as a result of the fact that Roman
prostitutes often served male clients
underneath the arches of the Colosseum.*

French

C'est une banane dans ta poche ou tu es juste content
de me voir?

Set oon banane don ta posh oo too eh juste conton
duh muh vwoir?

✳

Spanish

¿Llevas un plátano en el bolsillo o es
que te alegras de verme?

Yeh-bahs oon plah-tah-noh ehn ehl bohl-see-yoh oh ehs
keh teh ah-leh-grahs deh behr-meh?

✳

Italian

Hai una banana in tasca o sei solo contento
di vedermi?

Aee oo-na ba-nana een ta-ska o say so-lo kon-taynto
dee vay-dayrmee?

✳

German

Ist das eine Banane in deiner Tasche oder freust
du dich so, mich zu sehen?

Ist das eye-neuh banan-eh in dye-ner tashe oder froist
doo dish zo, mish tsu sehen?

✳

Finnish

Onks sulla banaani taskussa vai oletko vain iloinen
mun näkemisestä?

Onks soolla banaani taskoossa vai oletko vayin iloynen
moon nakemisesta?

'The bed is comfier than the sofa.'

French
Le lit est plus confortable que le canapé.
Luh lee eh ploo confortabluh kuh luh canapay.

Spanish
La cama es más cómoda que el sofá.
La kah-mah ehs mahs koh-moh-dah keh ehl soh-fah.

Italian
Il letto è più comodo del divano.
Eel layt-to e peeyoo ko-modo dayl dee-vano.

German
Das Bett ist bequemer als das Sofa.
Das bet ist beqvemer als das sofa.

Czech
Postel je pohodlnější než pohovka.
Postel ye pohodolnyeyshee nezh pohofka.

Global Sex Fact

The ankh or Egyptian cross is a symbol representing sexuality and eternal life. The cross represents the penis and testicles, whilst the oval above it represents the vagina.

French
Tu as été une méchante fille / un méchant garçon.
Maintenant file dans ma chambre!
Too a etay oon meshonte fee / un meshon garson.
Mantuhnon fill don ma shombruh!

✳

Spanish
Has sido una chica mala / un chico malo.
¡Vete a mi habitación!
Ahs see-doh oo-nah chee-kah mah-lah / oon chee-koh
mah-loh. Beh-teh ah mee ah-bee-tah-thee-ohn!

✳

Italian
Sei stata / stato disubbidiente. Adesso va in camera mia!
Sayee sta-ta / sta-to deesoob-beedeeayn-tay.
Adays-so va een ka-mayra mee-a!

✳

German
Du warst ein sehr unartiges Mädchen / ein sehr
unartiger Junge. Geh in mein Zimmer!
Doo varst ine zehr oonarti-ges maydshen / ine zehr
oonarti-ger yoon-ge. Geh in mine tsimer!

✳

Russian
Ты былá óчень плохóй дéвочкой (*to a woman*) / Ты был
óчень плохúм мáльчиком (*to a man*). А тепéрь марш в мою
кóмнату!'
Ty byla ochini plahoy dievachkay (to a woman) / Ty byl ochini
plahim malichikam (to a man). A tiperi marsh v mayoo
komnatoo!

French
Suce le, pour voir?
Soos luh, pour vwoir?

✱

Spanish
Chupa un ratito.
Choo-pah oon rrah-tee-toh.

✱

Italian
Succhialo per un po'.
Sookeea-lo payr oo-n po.

✱

German
Lutsch ihn eine Weile.
Lootsh een eye-neuh vile-euh.

✱

Thai
ดูดตรงนั้นสักพัก
Dood trong nun sak pak.

Global Sex Fact

In ancient Rome the penis symbolized good fortune. A phallus was often carved on the doorways of Roman houses to bring prosperity to those who dwelt there.

French
Et si on t'enlevait ces fringues mouillées?
Ay see on tonlevay say frang mooweeay?

*

Spanish
Déjame que te quite esa ropa mojada.
Deh-hah-meh keh teh kee-teh eh-sah rro-pah moh-hah-dah.

*

Italian
Adesso togliamo questi vestiti bagnati.
Adays-so to-lyeeamo kwe-stee vay-steetee banya-tee.

*

German
Komm, ich helf dir aus deinen nassen Sachen.
Kom, ish helf deer ous dye-nen nassen sakhen.

*

Hindi
चलो, अब ये तुम्हारे गीले कपड़े उतार देते हैं।
Chalo, ab toomhare geele kapde ootaar dete hain.

Global Sex Fact

In Polynesia it is usual practice for both male and female adolescents to receive instruction in sexual technique by an experienced older person.

French
Mes sous-vêtements sont comestibles.
May soovetmon son comesteebluh.

✻

Spanish
Mi ropa interior es comestible.
Mee rroh-pah een-teh-ree-ohr ehs koh-mehs-tee-bleh.

✻

Italian
Le mie mutande sono commestibili.
Lay mee-ay moo-tanday so-no com-maystee-beelee.

✻

German
Meine Unterwäsche ist essbar.
Mye-neuh oonter-vesheuh ist essbar.

✻

Hebrew
התחתונים שלי אכילים.
Hatakhtonim sheli akhilim.

Global Sex Fact

Females brought up on the island of Lesu are said to entice male interest by displaying their genitals to the object of their desire.

French
Je ne porte pas de sous-vêtements.
Juh nuh port pa duh soovetmon.

*

Spanish
No estoy usando ninguna ropa interior.
Noh ehs-toh-ee oo-sand-oh nin-goon-ah roh-pah in-terr-y-or.

*

Italian
Non indosso le mutande.
Non eendos-so lay moo-tanday.

*

German
Ich trage keine Unterwäsche
Ish traa-ger kine-eh oonter-vesheuh.

*

Korean
저 속옷 안 입고 있어요.
Jeu sog-ot ahn ib-go it-sseu-yo.

Global Sex Fact

Polyandry is practised by the Toda of India. When a female marries she becomes wife to all of her husband's brothers and establishes a sexual relationship with all of them.

'Do they have banana flavoured?'

French
Ça existe, saveur banane?
Sa exeest, saveur banan?

∗

Spanish
¿Lo tienen con sabor a plátano?
Loh tee-eh-nehn cohn sah-bohr ah plah-tah-noh?

∗

Italian
Ne hanno al gusto di banana?
Nay an-no al goo-sto dee ba-nana?

∗

German
Gibt's die auch mit Bananengeschmack?
Gibt-s dee oukh meet bananen-geshmaack?

∗

Thai
มีรสชาดกล้วยไหม
Mee rotchaat gluay mai?

Global Sex Fact

_In the 2005 Durex Global Sex Survey,
lovers in Belgium and Poland topped
the contentment chart, whilst the Chinese
and Japanese were the least happy
with their sex lives._

'Make love to me.'

French
Fais-moi l'amour.
Fay mwah lamore.

✻

Spanish
Hazme el amor.
Ahth-meh ehl ah-mohr.

✻

Italian
Facciamo l'amore.
Facheea-mo lamo-ray.

✻

German
Schlaf mit mir.
Shlarf mit meer.

✻

Swedish
Ligg med mig.
Ligg mied mey.

✻

Dutch
Vrij met me.
Vrey met meu.

French

**As-tu apporté assez de crème anglaise pour remplir
la baignoire?**

*A too aportay assay duh crem onglaze pour rompleer
la bainwoire?*

✳

Spanish

**¿Has traído suficiente nata para
llenar la bañera?**

*Ahs trah-ee-doh soo-phee-thee-ehn-teh nah-tah pah-rah
yeh-nahr la bah-nee-eh-rah?*

✳

Italian

**Hai portato abbbastanza crema per riempire
la vasca da bagno?**

*Aee porta-to ab-bastan-za kre-ma payr reeaympee-ray
la va-sca da ba-nyo?*

✳

German

Hast du genug Pudding, um das Bad zu füllen?

Hast doo genoog pooding, oom das bad tsoo foollen?

✳

Czech

Máš dost pudinku, abysme jím naplnili vanu?

Maash dost poodinkoo, abisme yim naplnili vanoo?

Sex

French
Le bâton s'est cassée. On a besoin d'une pince à épiler.
Luh baton seh cassay. On a bezwon doon panse a epelay.

Spanish
La caña se ha roto.
Necesitamos unas pinzas.
La kah-nee-ah seh ah rroh-toh.
Neh-theh-see-tah-mohs oo-nahs peen-thahs.

Italian
Il bastone si è frantumato.
Abbiamo bisogno delle pinzette.
Eel basto-nay see e frantoo-mato.
Ab-beeamo bee-sonyo dayl-lay peen-tsayt-tay.

German
Der Stock ist zersplittert. Wir brauchen eine Pinzette.
Der shtock ist tsershplitert. Veer broukhen eye-neuh pintsette.

Global Sex Fact

If a Goajiro woman of Colombia is successful in tripping up a man during a ceremonial dance, he is required to have sex with her.

French
***Reste comme ça pendant que je vais chercher
le saucisson.***
*Rest com sa pondon kuh juh vay shershay
luh sosseeson.*

Spanish
***No te muevas de esta postura
mientras coloco la salchicha.***
*Noh teh moo-eh-bahs deh ehs-tah pohs-too-rah
mee-ehn-trahs koh-loh-koh la sahl-chee-chah.*

Italian
***Resta in questa posizione mentre vado
a prendere il salame.***
*Ray-sta een kwe-sta poseetseeo-nay mayn-tray va-do
a prayn-dayray eel sala-may.*

German
Beweg dich nicht, ich hol die Salami.
Beveg deesh nisht, ish hol dee salami.

*

Czech
Zůstaň tak, než dodám salám.
Zoostany tak, nezh dodaam salaam.

'Take care, my gynaecologist lost his wrist watch.'

French

Fais gaffe, mon gynéco y a perdu sa montre.

Fay gaff, mon gyneko e a pairdoo sa montruh.

Spanish

**Ten cuidado, por ahí perdió
el reloj mi ginecólogo.**

*Tehn koo-eeh-dah-doh, pohr ah-ee pehr-dee-oh
ehl rreh-lohh mee hee-neh-koh-loh-goh.*

Italian

**Fa attenzione, il mio ginecologo
ci ha perso l'orologio.**

*Fa at-tayn-tseeonay, eel mee-o jeenay-kologo
chee a payr-so loro-lojoe.*

German

**Pass auf, mein Gynäkologe hat seine
Armbanduhr verloren.**

*Pass ouf, mine gye-nakolo-geuh hat zine-neuh
armbandoohr ferloren.*

Russian

Осторо́жно, мой гинеко́лог потеря́л с руки́ часы́.

Astarozhna, moy ginikolag patiryal s rooki chasy.

French
Bien sûr que ton ami / amie peut se joindre à nous.
Be-en sur kuh ton amee peuh suh jwoindruh a noo.

*

Spanish
***Pues claro que puede participar
tu amigo / amiga.***
*Poo-ehs klah-roh keh poo-eh-deh pahr-tee-thee-pahr
too ah-mee-goh / ah-mee-gah.*

*

Italian
***Naturalmente che il tuo amico / amica può
unirsi a noi.***
*Natooral-mayntay ke eel too-o amee-ko / amee-ka pwo
ooneer-see a no-ee.*

*

German
Natürlich kann dein Freund / deine Freundin mitmachen.
Natoorlish kan dine froind / dye-neuh froindin mitmakhen.

*

Hindi
बिल्कुल, तुम्हारी सहेली भी शामिल हो सकती है।
Bilkool, toomhari saheli bhi shaamil ho sakti hai.

French
Le dernier arrivé est le gagnant!
Luh durne-ay arreevay eh luh ganyant!

✳

Spanish
¡El último que llegue gana!
Ehl ool-tee-moh keh yeh-gheh gah-nah!

✳

Italian
L'ultimo che arriva è il vincitore!
Lool-teemo ke ar-ree-va e eel veenchee-toray!

✳

German
Wer zuletzt kommt, hat gewonnen!
Ver tsuletst komt, hat gevonnen!

✳

Hebrew
!האחרון זוכה
Ha-akharon zokhe!

Essential Vocabulary

Orgasm, *noun*

French ***orgasme***
Spanish ***orgasmo***
Italian ***orgasmo***
German ***Orgasmus, Höhepunkt***

French
Où est-ce que je peux trouver un dauphin à cette heure-ci?
Oo es-kuh juh peuh troovay un dofan a set eur-see?

✳

Spanish
**¿Dónde puedo encontrar una buena
tranca a estas horas de la noche?**
*Doh-deh poo-eh-doh ehn-kohn-trrahr oo-nah boo-eh-nah
trrahn-kah ah ehs-ahs oh-rahs deh la noh-cheh?*

✳

Italian
**Dove posso trovare un delfino a quest'ora
di notte?**
*Do-vay pos-so tro-varay oo-n dayl-feeno a kwe-stora
dee not-tay?*

✳

German
Wo bekomme ich um diese Zeit noch einen Delfin?
Vo bekom-meuh ish oom dee-zeuh tsite nokh eye-nen delfin?

✳

Korean
이 밤에 돌고래를 어디서 얻을 수
있나요?
Ih bam-e dol-go-rae-reul eu-di-seu eu-deul soo it-na-yo?

'If you're going to regret this in the morning, we can sleep in till the afternoon.'

French
Si tu vas le regretter demain matin, on peut dormir jusqu'à midi.
See too va luh regrettay duhman matan, on peuh dormeer juska midi.

Spanish
Si vas a arrepentirte de esto por la mañana, podemos seguir durmiendo hasta el mediodía.
See bahs ah ah-rreh-pehn-teer-teh deh ehs-toh pohr la mah-nee-ah-nah, poh-deh-mohs seh-gheehr door-mee-ehn-doh ahs-tah ehl meh-dee-oh-dee-ah.

Italian
Se domani mattina lo rimpiangerai, possiamo dormire fino al pomeriggio.
Say doma-nee mat-teena lo reempeean-jayraee pos-seeamo dor-meeray fee-no al po-mayree-joe.

German
Wenn du es am Morgen bereust, können wir bis in den Nachmittag hinein schlafen.
Ven doo es am morgan beroist, keunnen veer bis in den nakhmeetag hin-ine shlafen.

Thai
ถ้าคุณยังไม่อยากตื่น เราสามารถนอนจนถึงบ่ายได้
Ta khoon yang mai yak deun rao samaat non jon teung bai dai.

French
Ils ne vont jamais me croire demain, au boulot.
Il nuh von jamay muh crwah duhman, o boolo.

✳

Spanish
Los del trabajo no se lo creerán
cuando se lo cuente mañana.
Lohs dehl trrah-bah-hoh noh seh loh krreh-eh-rahn
koo-ahn-doh seh loh koo-ehn-teh mah-nee-ah-nah.

✳

Italian
Domani al lavoro non mi crederanno mai.
Do-manee al la-voro non mee kre-dayran-no ma-ee.

✳

German
Auf der Arbeit glaubt mir das morgen keiner.
Ouf der ar-bite gloubt meer das morgan kye-ner.

✳

Dutch
Dat geloven m'n collega's morgen nooit.
Dat gelovun mun colleygahs morgun noyt.

Global Sex Fact

*Anal sex was common practice in ancient
Rome, and in ancient Greece high-class
prostitutes often insisted on it.*

French
Garde le rythme en chantant 'Dancing Queen'.
Garde luh rythme on shonton 'Dancing Queen'.

✻

Spanish
Ahora, para no perder el ritmo,
canta 'Dancing Queen'.
Ah-oh-rah, pah-rah noh pehr-dehr ehl rreet-moh,
kahn-tah mah-ree-kee-tah peh-rehth.

✻

Italian
Adesso mantieni il ritmo cantando
'Dancing Queen'.
Adays-so manteeay-nee eel ree-tmo kan-tando
'Dancing Queen'.

✻

German
Und jetzt halte den Rhythmus.
Sing einfach 'Dancing Queen'.
Oond jetst hal-teuh den rootmoos.
Sing ine-fakh 'Dancing Queen'.

✻

Danish
Og hold så rytmen ved at synge 'Dancing Queen'.
Oh hold so rootmen ve a soonge 'Dancing Queen'.

'Pass the baby oil, please.'

French
Passe-moi l'huile de massage, s'il te plaît.
Pass mwah lu-ee duh massaje, sil tuh play.

✳

Spanish
***Pásame el aceite de bebé,
por favor.***
*Pah-sah-meh ehl ah-theh-ee-teh deh beh-beh,
pohr phah-bohrr.*

✳

Italian
Mi passi l'olio per il corpo per favore?
Mee pas-see lo-leeo payr eel kor-po payr fa-voray?

✳

German
Gib mir bitte das Babyöl.
Geeb meer bit-teuh das baby-eul.

Global Sex Fact

The term 'homosexual' is said to have first been used in 1869 by a Hungarian researcher called Bonkert.

'This is a real maid's outfit.
I've locked her in the cupboard.'

French
Ceci est une vrai tenue de bonne.
Elle, je l'ai enfermée dans le placard.
Suh-see et oon vray tenoo duh bonn.
Ell, juh lay onfairmay don luh plackard.

✳

Spanish
Éste es un traje auténtico de camarera.
He encerrado a la dueña en el armario.
Ehs-teh ehs oon trah-heh ah-oo-tehn-tee-koh
deh kah-mah-reh-rah. Eh ehn-theh-rrah-doh
ah la doo-eh-nee-ah ehn ehl ahr-mah-ree-oh.

✳

Italian
Questa è un'autentica divisa da domestica.
Lei, l'ho chiusa nell'armadio.
Kwe-sta e oon-awtayn-teeka dee-veesa da do-maysteeka.
Lay, lo keeoo-sa nayl-larma-deeo.

✳

German
Das ist eine echte Zimmermädchenuniform.
Ich habe sie hier in den Schrank gesperrt.
Das eest ine-euh eshte tsimer-maydshen-ooniform.
Ish ha-beuh zee heer in den shrank ge-shpert.

'Yes, we can do it in the car,

but I'm not slowing down.'

French
Oui, on peut le faire dans la voiture,
mais je ne ralentis pas.
Wee, on peuh luh faire don la vwoiture,
may juh nuh rallontee pa.

✳

Spanish
Claro que podemos hacerlo en el coche,
pero no pienso ir más despacio.
Klah-roh keh poh-deh-mohs ah-thehr-loh ehn ehl koh-cheh,
peh-roh noh pee-ehn-soh eer mahs dehs-pah-thee-oh.

✳

Italian
Certo che possiamo farlo in macchina,
però io non rallento.
Cher-to ke pos-seeamo far-lo een ma-keena,
pay-ro eeo non ral-laynto.

✳

German
Ja, wir können's im Auto machen,
aber ich werde dabei nicht langsamer.
Ya, veer keunen-s im outo makhen,
aber ish ver-deuh da-bye nisht lungsamer.

French
Tu es encore plus chaude que ta sœur . . . et ta mère.
Too eh onkore ploo showd kuh ta seur . . . et ta mare.

✳

Spanish
Eres más cachonda que tu hermana . . .
y que tu madre.
Eh-rehs mahs kah-chohn-dah keh too ehr-mah-nah . . .
ee keh too mah-dreh.

✳

Italian
Sei anche più vogliosa di tua sorella . . .
e di tua madre.
Say an-ke peeyoo volyee-osa dee too-a sorayl-la . . .
ay dee too-a ma-dray.

✳

German
Du bist noch heißer als deine Schwester . . .
und deine Mutter.
Doo bist nokh hye-ser als dye-neuh shvester . . .
oond dye-neuh mooter.

✳

Hindi
तुम बिस्तर में अपनी बहन से भी ज़्यादा गर्म हो, . . . और अपनी मां से
भी ।
Toom bister mein apnee behan se bhi zyaada garm ho, . . .
aur apnee maan se bhi.

French
Zorro ne quitte jamais son masque et ses eperons.
Zorro nuh keet jamay son mask ay ses ep-er-on.

Spanish
**El Llanero Solitario siempre lleva
puestas una máscara y un par
de espuelas.**
Ehl yah-neh-roh soh-lee-tah-ree-oh see-ehm-preh yeh-bah
poo-ehs-tahs oo-nah mahs-kah-rah ee oon pahr
deh ehs-poo-eh-lahs.

Italian
Zorro non toglie mai la maschera e gli speroni.
Dzor-ro non to-liay maee la ma-skera ay lee spayronee.

German
Der einsame Cowboy trägt stets Maske und Sporen.
Der ine-zaa-meuh cowboy traygt shtets mas-keuh oond
shpo-ren.

Hebrew
הפרש הבודד לובש תמיד מסכה ודורבנות.
Ha-parash ha-boded lovesh tamid masekha oo-dorbanot.

French

***Qui aurait crû qu'on puisse se mettre à deux
sur ce monocycle?***

*Kee oaray croo kon pweece suh mettruh a deuh
soor suh monoseekluh?*

Spanish

***¿Quién hubiera dicho que podían
ir dos en un monociclo?***

*Kee-ehn oo-bee-eh-rah dee-choh keh poh-dee-ahn
eer dohs ehn oon moh-noh-thee-kloh?*

Italian

***Chi avrebbe pensato che due persone potessero
stare su questo monociclo?***

*Kee avrayb-bay payn-sato ke doo-ay payr-sonay potays-sayro
staa-ray soo kwe-sto mono-cheeclo?*

German

Wer hätte gedacht, dass zwei auf ein Einrad passen?

Ver het-te gedakht, dass tsvye ouf ine ine-rad passen?

✳

Thai

ใครว่าคุณสามารถเข้าไปในยูนิไซค์เคิลได้สองคน

Krai wa khoon samaat kao bai nai unicycle dai song khon.

French

*Ça plaîrait pas à ta mère, ça. D'ailleurs quand j'y pense,
ça ne lui a pas plû.*

Sa plairay paz a ta mare, sa. Diyeur cond jee ponce,
sa nuh lwee a pa ploo.

Spanish

*A tu madre esto no le gustaría nada.
La verdad es que no le gustó
en absoluto.*

Ah too mah-dreh ehs-toh noh leh goos-tah-ree-ah nah-dah.
La behr-dahd ehs keh noh leh goos-toh
ehn ahb-soh-loo-toh.

Italian

*A tua madre questo non piacerebbe,
infatti non le è piaciuto.*

A too-a ma-dray kwe-sto non peea-cherayb-be,
een-fat-tee non lay e peea-chyouto.

German

*Deiner Mutter würde das nicht gefallen.
Wenn ich's recht bedenke, es gefiel ihr überhaupt nicht.*

Dye-ner mooter voorde das nisht gefallen.
Ven ish-s resht be-den-keuh, es gefeel eer uberhoupt nisht.

✳

Danish

*Det her ville din mor ikke bryde sig om.
Og det gjorde hun faktisk ikke.*

Dey her vil deen mor ik broo sigh om.
Og dey gyor hoon faktisk igge.

French
C'est légal en Lituanie.
Seh legal on Litooanee.

Spanish
Es legal en Lituania.
Ess lehgal ehn Litooania.

Italian
È legale in Lituania.
E lay-galay een Lee-too-aneea.

German
In Litauen ist dass legal.
In Litowen ist das laygarl.

Finnish
Tämä on laillista Liettuassa.
Tama on laelista lihtuasa.

Essential Vocabulary

Breasts, *noun*

French **seins**
Spanish **pechos**
Italian **seno**, **tette**
German **Brüsten**, **Titten**

French
Je ne savais pas qu'on pouvait ouvrir une bouteille de vodka comme ça.

Juh nuh savay pa kon poovay oovrear oon bootay duh vodka comm sa.

✳

Spanish
No sabía yo que pudieras abrir las botellas de vodka con eso.

Noh sah-bee-ah yoh keh poo-dee-eh-rahs ah-breer lahs boh-teh-yahs deh bohth-kah kohn eh-soh.

✳

Italian
Non sapevo che si potesse aprire una bottiglia di vodka così.

Non sa-payvo ke see potays-say apree-ray oo-na bot-tilya di vo-dka ko-zi.

✳

German
Ich wusste nie, dass man so eine Wodkaflasche öffnen kann.

Ish vooster nee, das man so eye-neuh Vodkaflasher eughffnen can.

✳

Russian
Я никогда́ не ду́мал (*male speaker*) / ду́мала (*female speaker*), что ты мо́жешь так откры́ть буты́лку во́дки.

Ya nikagda neeh doomal (male speaker) / doomala (female speaker), shto ty mozhesh tak akryti bootylkoo vodki.

French
Mets le masque de Margaret Thatcher, s'il te plaît.
May luh mask duh Margaret Thatcher, sil tuh play.

Spanish
**¡Anda, ponte la máscara
de Margaret Thatcher!**
*Ahn-dah, pohn-teh la mahs-kah-rah
deh Mahr-gah-reht Tah-chehr!*

Italian
Indossa la maschera di Margaret Thatcher, per favore!
Eendos-sa la ma-skera dee Margaret Thatcher, payr fa-voray!

German
Bitte setz dich die Margaret Thatcher Maske auf.
Bitter sets dish dee Margaret Thatcher mass-keuh ouf.

Russian
Пожáлуйста, надéнь мáску Мáргарет Тэтчер.
Pazhaloosta, nadeni maskoo Margaret Tetcher.

Global Sex Fact

*Male inhabitants of the Western Caroline
Islands are said to sing to their partners
before and after sexual intercourse.*

'My phone can send this picture to your friends.'

French
Mon portable peut envoyer cette photo à tes amis.
Mon portabluh peuh onvoyay set image a tez amee.

Spanish
**Mi teléfono puede enviar esta
foto a todos tus amigos.**
*Mee teh-leh-phoh-noh poo-eh-deh ehn-bee-ahr ehs-tah
phoh-toh ah toh-dohs toos ah-mee-gohs.*

Italian
**Il mio telefononino può inviare questa foto
ai tuoi amici.**
*Eel mee-o taylay-fon-eeno pwo een-veearay kwe-sta fo-to
aee too-oee amee-chee.*

German
**Ich kann das Bild mit meinem Handy an deine Freunde
schicken.**
*Ick can dass Billt mitt mine-em Handy an diner Froyn-deuh
shicken.*

Hindi
मेरा मोबाइल यह तस्वीरें तुम्हारे लोगों को भेज सकता है।
*Mera mobile yeh tasveer toomhaare doston ko bhej
saktaa hai.*

'I'd like a bowl of water for my gimp, please.'

French

Je pourrais avoir un bol d'eau pour mon esclave sexuel, s'il vous plaît?

Juh pouray avwoir un bol deau pour mon eslaav sexuel, sil voo play?

✳

Spanish

Quisiera, por favor, una palangana de agua para mi esclavo.

Kee-see-eh-rah, pohr pha-bohrr, oo-nah pah-lahn-gah-nah deh ah-goo-ah pah-rah mee ehs-klah-boh.

✳

Italian

Vorrei una ciotola d'acqua per il mio schiavo, per favore.

Vor-rayee oo-na cheeo-tola da-kwa payr eel mee-o skeea-vo, payr fa-voray.

✳

German

Ich möchte einen Napfwasser für meinen Sklave bitte.

Ish mershter eye-nen napfvasser fyour my-nen sklarver bitter.

✳

Korean

내 노예를 위해 물 한 사발이 필요해요.

Nae no-ye-reul wi-hae mool han sa-ba-ri pi-ryo-hae-yo.

French
Ciel, ma femme / mon mari! Vite, dans le placard!
Se-el, ma famm / mon maree! Veet, don luh plackard!

✳

Spanish
¡Mi mujer / marido. Rápido,
al armario!
Mee moo-hehr / mah-ree-doh. Rrah-pee-doh,
ahl ahr-mah-ree-oh!

✳

Italian
Presto, mio marito / mia moglie! Nell'armadio!
Pray-sto, mee-o maree-to / mee-a mo-lyay! Nayl-larma-deeo.

✳

German
Schnell, meine Frau / mein Mann!
Auf in den Kleiderschrank!
Sshnell, my-neuh Frow / mine Mann!
Ouf in dayn Kleyedurschrank!

✳

Swedish
Fort! Min hustru / mann! In i garderaben!
Foort! Min hustru / mann! In ee garderuoben!

✳

Thai
เร็ว เมีย/สามีมา เข้าไปในตู้เลย
Raew, mia / samii ma! Khao bai nai dto loey!

French
Ça fait un moment que je n'ai pas vu le hamster.
Sa fay un momon kuh juh nay pa voo luh amster.

✻

Spanish
Hace tiempo que no veo el conejito.
Ah-theh tee-ehm-poh keh noh beh-oh ehl koh-neh-hee-toh.

✻

Italian
Non vedo il criceto da un po'.
Non vay-do eel kree-cheto da oo-n po.

✻

German
Ich habe den Hamster schon lange nicht mehr gesehen.
Ish ha-beuh den hamster shon lang-euh nisht mer gesehen.

✻

Dutch
Ik heb de hamster al een tijdje niet gezien.
Ik heb deuh hahmster al eun teydjuh neet guzeen.

Essential Vocabulary

Penis, *noun*

French **pénis**
Spanish **pene**
Italian **cazzo, uccello**
German **Penis, männliche Glied**

French
Ouvre grand.
Ouvruh gron.

✳

Spanish
Ábrete bien.
Ah-breh-teh bee-ehn.

✳

Italian
Apri bene.
Apree bay-nay.

✳

German
Weit geöffnet.
Vyte guhuffnut.

✳

Hindi
पूरा खोलो ।
Poora kholo.

Global Sex Fact

During ceremonies of puberty which feature male circumcision, the Australian Aborigines exchange wives as a sign of friendship and goodwill.

'Does this need special batteries?'

French
Ça nécessite des batteries spéciales, ce machin?
Sa neseseet day batteree spese-al, suh mashan?

*

Spanish
¿Esto lleva pilas especiales?
Ehs-toh yeh-bah pee-lahs ehs-peh-thee-ah-lehs?

*

Italian
Ha bisogno di batterie speciali?
A bee-sonyo dee bat-tayreeay spay-cheealee?

*

German
Braucht man besondere Batterien dafür?
Browcht man buhsonnderer batteree-en darfyour?

*

Danish
Skal der særlige batterier til den her?
Skal der sairliye batteriye te den hair?

Essential Vocabulary

Bottom, *noun*

French **derrière**
Spanish **trasero**, **traste**
Italian **sedere**, **posteriore**, **culo**
German **Arsch**, **Po**

French
J'ai trois voies d'accès.
Jay twah vwah dacksay.

✳

Spanish
Tengo tres puertos de entrada.
Tehn-goh trehs poo-ehr-tohs deh ehn-trah-dah.

✳

Italian
Ho tre entrate.
Oh tray entra-tay.

✳

German
Ich habe drei Eingänge.
Ish ha-beuh drye ine-geng-euh.

✳

Korean
제게는 항구가 세 개 있어요.
Je-gae-neun hang-goo-ga se-gae it-seu-yo.

Global Sex Fact

Ancient Egyptian women are said to have created tampons from softened papyrus, whilst Roman women favoured wads of wool.

French
Allonge-toi et pense à la France.
Allonge twah ay ponce a la patrie.

*

Spanish
Túmbate y piensa en España.
Toom-bah-teh ee pee-ehn-sah ehn Ehs-pah-nee-ah.

*

Italian
Sdraiati e pensa all'Italia.
Sdraeea-tee ay payn-sa al-leeta-leea.

*

German
Leg dich hin und denk an Deutschland.
Layg dish hin oont denk an Doytshlant.

*

Finnish
Silmät vaan kiinni ja ajattele isänmaata.
Silmat vaan kiinni ya ayattele isanmaata.

Global Sex Fact

*It was the custom of some Romans to
demand the deflowering of a virgin before
marriage with the wooden phallus of
the fertility god.*

French
**Tu es le premier Français / la première Française
que je me tape.**
Too eh luh prem-e-air Fransay / la premiaire Fransaize
kuh juh muh tape.

Spanish
**Eres la primera persona española
que me he tirado.**
Eh-rehs la pree-meh-rah pehr-soh-nah ehs-pah-nee-oh-lah
keh meh eh tee-rah-doh.

Italian
**Sei il primo italiano / la prima italiana
con il / la quale ho fatto l'amore.**
Say eel pree-mo eeta-leeano / la pree-ma eeta-leeanea
kon eel / la kwa-lay oh fat-to lamo-ray.

German
**Du bist der / die erste Deutsche mit wem
ich je geschlafen habe.**
Doo biss-t dare / dee airster Doyt-cheuh mitt veym
ish yay geshlarfen ha-beuh.

Czech
Jsi první Čech (to a male), **kterého jsem měla**
(female speaker). **Jsi první Češka** (to a female),
kterou jsem měl (male speaker).
Ysi prvnyee Chekh (to a male), kstereho jsem mnyela
(female speaker). Ysi prvnyee Cheshka (to a female),
kteroo jsem mnyel (male speaker).

French
Oui! Oui! Oui!
Wee! Wee! Wee!

✳

Spanish
¡Si! ¡Si! ¡Si!
See! See! See!

✳

Italian
Si! Si! Si!
See! See! See!

✳

German
Ja! Ja! Ja!
Yar! Yar! Yar!

✳

Russian
Да! Да! Да!
Dah! Dah! Dah!

Global Sex Fact

In Victorian England there were special houses where unmarried women could spend their pregnancies in secret.

After Sex

French

Il faut qu'on s'arrête, je ne sens plus mes jambes.

Ill foh kon sarett, juh son ploo may jomb.

✳

Spanish

Tenemos que parar. Se me ha dormido
todo de cintura para abajo.

Teh-neh-mohs keh pah-rahr. Seh meh ah dohrr-mee-doh
toh-doh deh theen-too-rah pah-rah ah-bah-hoh.

✳

Italian

Dobbiamo smettere. Non sento più le mie gambe.

Dob-e-amo smay-te-ree. Non sent-o pyoo le me-ay gamb-ay.

✳

German

Wir müssen aufhören. Unterhalb der Hüfte
habe ich alles Gefühl verloren.

Veer moossen oufheuren. Oonterhalb der hoofte
ha-beuh ish al-les gefoohl ferloren.

✳

Hindi

हमें रुकना पड़ेगा। मेरा नीचे वाला भाग सुन्न हो गया है।

Hoomein rookna padhega. Mera neeche waala bhaag
soonn ho gayaa hai.

French

Je t'enverrai les clès des menottes quand je rentre chez moi.

Juh tonverray lay clay day menott kon juh rontruh shay mwah.

Spanish

**Te enviaré por correo las llaves
de las esposas cuando vuelva a casa.**

*Teh ehn-bee-ah-reh pohr koh-rreh-oh lahs yah-behs
deh lahs ehs-poh-sahs koo-ahn-doh boo-ehl-bah ah kah-sah.*

Italian

**Ti invio per posta le chiavi delle manette
appena torno a casa.**

*Tee een-veeo payr po-sta lay keea-vee dayl-lay ma-nayt-tay
ap-pay-na tor-no a ka-za.*

German

**Ich steck die Schlüssel für die Handschellen in die Post,
sobald ich wieder zu Hause bin.**

*Ish shtek dee shloossel foor dee hand-shelen in dee post,
sobald ish veeder tsu house-euh bin.*

Hebrew

אשלח את מפתחות האזיקים בדואר, כשאחזור
הביתה.

*Eshlakh et maftekhot ha-azykim ba-doar,
kshe-akhzor habayta.*

French
Vite, ils sont en train de fermer les grilles du parc.
Veet, ils sont on tran duh fermay lay gree du park.

Spanish
**Date prisa, están cerrando la entrada
del parque.**
*Dah-teh pree-sah, ehs-tahn theh-rrahn-doh la ehn-trah-dah
dehl pahr-keh.*

*

Italian
Presto, stanno chiudendo il cancello del parco.
Pray-sto, stan-no kyou-dayndo eel kan-chel-lo dayl par-ko.

*

German
Schnell, sie schliessen das Parktor ab.
Shnell, zee shleessen dass parktor ap.

Essential Vocabulary

To shag, *verb*

French **baiser**
Spanish **tirar, follar**
Italian **scopare, trombare, fottere**
German **ficken, bumsen**

French
Tu prends les cartes de crédit?
Too pron lay cart duh credeet?

✳

Spanish
¿Aceptas tarjetas de crédito?
Ah-thep-tahs tahr-heh-tahs deh kreh-dee-toh?

✳

Italian
Accetti la carta di credito?
Achet-tee la kar-ta dee kre-deeto?

✳

German
Kann ich mit Kreditkarte bezahlen?
Can ish mitt credeetcarter betsarlen?

✳

Korean
크레딧 카드 받나요?
Credit card bat-na-yo?

Global Sex Fact

The Taoists of China believed that every time a man ejaculated his yang energy was depleted.

French
Retourne-moi et recommence.
Ruhtourne-mwah ay ruhcommonse.

✳

Spanish
Dame la vuelta y házmelo otra vez.
Dah-meh la boo-ehl-tah ee ahth-meh-loh oh-trah behth.

✳

Italian
Girami e ricomincia.
Jee-ramee ay ree-komeen-cheea.

✳

German
Dreh mich um und mach's noch einmal.
Drey mish oom oond makh-s nokh ine-mal.

✳

Hebrew
גלגל אותי ובוא נעשה את זה שוב.
Galggel oti oo-bo naase et ze shuv.

Global Sex Fact

In seventeenth-century France female sexual excitement was sometimes considered a sign of mental illness.

French
On va jamais réussir à enlever toute cette gelée des draps!
On va jamay rayooseer a onlevay toot sett jellay day drap!

✳

Spanish
Nunca conseguirás quitar toda esta gelatina de las sábanas.
Noon-kah kohn-seh-gheeh-rahs kee-tahr toh-dah ehs-tah heh-lah-tee-nah deh lahs sah-bah-nahs.

✳

Italian
Non riusciremo mai a togliere tutta questa marmellata dalle lenzuola.
Non reeoo-sheeraymo maee a to-lieeray toot-ta kwe-sta mar-mayl-lata dal-lay layn-tsoo-ola.

✳

German
Wir werden nie dieses ganze Gelee von den Laken bekommen.
Veer verden nee deezes gantse dze-lee fon den laa-ken bekommen.

✳

Korean
이 시트의 젤리는 절대 지우지 못할거야.
Ih si-teu-eui jelly-neun jeul-tae ji-oo-ji mot-hal-keu-ya.

French
C'était sensationnel!
Settay sonsaseeonel!

✳

Spanish
¡Ha sido increíble!
Ah see-doh een-kreh-ee-bleh!

✳

Italian
È stato sensazionale!
E sta-to sayn-satseeona-lay!

✳

German
Das war unglaublich!
Dass varr unglaublish!

✳

Thai
มันเป็นรสชาดของชีวิต

Mun ben rotchaat khong cheewit!

Global Sex Fact

Instead of kissing, the Tinquian people of the Pacific islands place their lips closely to their partners and inhale.

French
La terre a tremblé?
La terr a tromblay?

✻

Spanish
¿Eso ha sido un terremoto?
Eh-soh ah see-doh oon teh-rreh-moh-toh?

✻

Italian
La terra si è mossa?
La tayr-ra see e mos-sa?

✻

German
Und, hat die Erde gebebt?
Oont, hat dee airder gebaybt?

✻

Dutch
Was het lekker?
Wass het lekker?

Global Sex Fact

The word 'buggery' has its roots in eleventh-century Bulgaria, the home of a Christian sect named the Bogomils who practised anal sex as a contraceptive precaution.

French
C'était comment pour toi?
Settay common pour twah?

∗

Spanish
¿Qué te ha parecido?
Keh teh ah pah-reh-thee-doh?

∗

Italian
Ti è piaciuto?
Tee e peeachyoo-to?

∗

German
Also, wie war es für dich?
Also, vee varr ess fur dish?

∗

Danish
Hvordan var det for dig?
Vordan var day for dye?

Global Sex Fact

In the late nineteenth century, high-class prostitutes in London were known as 'horse-breakers' because of their habit of riding in the city's more fashionable areas.

'Do you fancy a fag or shall we go again?'

French

Ça te dirait une clope ou on s'y remet tout de suite?

Sa tuh dearay oon clop oo on see ruhmay too duh sweet?

*

Spanish

¿Te apetece un pitillo o lo hacemos otra vez?

Teh ah-peh-teh-theh oon pee-tee-yoh oh loh ah-theh-mohs oh-trah behth?

*

Italian

Vuoi fumare una sigaretta o ricominciamo di nuovo?

Voo-oee foo-maray oo-na see-garayt-ta o ree-komeencheea-mo dee nwo-vo?

*

German

Wie wär's mit einer Zigarette oder sollen wir erst noch einmal?

Vee vayr-s mit ine-er tsigaret-te oder zollen veer erst nokh ine-mal?

*

Finnish

Pannaanko tupakaksi vai heti uusiksi?

Pannako toopakaksi vai heti ooseksi?

French
Ça m'a donné faim.
Sa ma donnay fam.

Spanish
Me ha entrado mucha hambre.
Meh ah ehn-trah-doh moo-chah ahm-breh.

Italian
Mi ha fatto venire fame.
Mee a fat-to vaynee-ray fa-may.

German
Das hat mich hungrig gemacht.
Dass hat mish hungrig gemackt.

Czech
Dostal (male speaker) / **dostala** (female speaker)
jsem z toho hlad.
*Dostal (male speaker) / dostala (female speaker)
ysem z toho hlad.*

Global Sex Fact

*In Aztec culture, avocados were considered
so sexually potent that virgins were
restricted from any contact with them.*

French
Je crois que l'oie ne se sent pas bien.
Juh crwah kuh lwah nuh suh sont pa be-an.

Spanish
Parece que la cosa ya no pita.
Pah-reh-theh keh la koh-sah yah noh pee-tah.

Italian
Credo che lo strozzapapere sia esausto.
Kre-do ke lo strodza-papayray see-a esow-sto.

German
***Ich glaube, die Gans braucht erst mal
eine Ruhepause.***
*Ish glou-beuh, dee gants broukht erst mal
ine-euh rooh-euh-pou-se.*

Essential Vocabulary

To rub, *verb*

French ***frotter***
Spanish ***frotar***
Italian ***fregare***
German ***einreiben***

French
Pourrais-tu me détacher maintenant, s'il te plaît?
Pouray too muh daytashay mantuhnon, sil tuh play?

✳

Spanish
¿Me desatas ya, por favor?
Meh dehs-ah-tahs yah, pohr fah-bohr?

✳

Italian
Mi sleghi ora, per favore?
Mee slay-gee o-ra, payr fa-voray?

✳

German
Kannst du mich jetzt bitte losbinden?
Canst doo mish yetst bitter lowsbindun?'

✳

Welsh
Elli di plîs ddatod fi nawr?
Elly dee please that odd vee nower?

✳

Portuguese
Quer desata-me agora?
Care desata-me agora?

✳

Swedish
Skulle du kunna binda loss mig nu!
Skulle doo kunna binda loss mey noo?

French
Tu es prêt / prête pour le deuxième round?
Too eh pray / pret pour luh deuzieme round?

*

Spanish
***¿Estás listo / lista para
el segundo asalto?***
*Ehs-tahs lees-toh / lees-tah pah-rah
ehl seh-goon-doh ah-sahl-toh?*

*

Italian
Sei pronto / pronta per il secondo round?
Say pron-to / pron-ta payr eel say-kondo round?

*

German
Bist du für die zweite Runde bereit?
Biss-t doo fyour dee zw-eye-teuh runder buh-right?

*

Hindi
तुम दूसरे राउंड के लिए तैयार हो?
Toom doosre round ke liye taiyaar ho?

Global Sex Fact

*Although Bangkok is now the unofficial sex
capital of the world, prostitution was
officially banned in Thailand in 1960.*

French
Je serai de nouveau prêt / prête dans une minute.
Juh seray duh noovoh pray / pret dons oon minoot.

Spanish
Estaré listo / lista dentro
de un momento.
Ehs-tah-reh lees-toh / lees-tah dehn-troh
deh oon moh-mehn-toh.

Italian
Sono pronto / pronta di nuovo tra un minuto.
So-no pron-to / pron-ta dee noo-ovo tra oo-n mee-nooto.

German
Ich bin gleich wieder bereit.
Ish bin glike veeder buh-right

Hebrew
אהיה מוכן שוב בתוך דקה.
Ehye mukhan shuv be-tokh daka.

Global Sex Fact

In 1994 a man was arrested in Arizona
for trying to solicit oral sex from a horse.

French
Laisse-moi récupérer mon souffle.
Lace mwah recuperay mon soofluh.

*

Spanish
Déjame que recobre el aliento.
Deh-hah-meh keh rreh-coh-breh ehl ah-lee-ehn-toh.

*

Italian
Lasciami riprendere fiato.
Lasheea-mee ree-praynday-ray feea-to.

*

German
Lass mich einmal Luft holen.
Lass mish ine-mal looft holen.

*

Korean
숨 좀 돌리구요
Soom jom dol-li-goo-yo.

Global Sex Fact

Julia the Elder, daughter of the Roman Emperor Augustus is thought to have had around 80,000 lovers.

French
Je ne dors pas sur la partie mouillée.
Juh nuh dor pa soor la partee mwouillay.

Spanish
Yo no duermo encima
de este charco.
Yoh noh doo-ehr-moh ehn-thee-mah
deh ehs-teh chahrr-koh.

Italian
Non dormo sulla chiazza bagnata.
Non dor-mo sool-la kia-dza ba-neeata.

German
Ich schlafe nicht auf der nassen Stelle.
Ish shla-feuh nisht ouf der nassen shtel-leuh.

Thai
ฉันจะไม่นอนบนพื้นเปียก
Chan ja mai non bon puen biaak.

Global Sex Fact

In ancient China oral sex was known
as 'mouth music'.

The Morning After

French
Qui es tu?
Kee eh too?

✻

Spanish
¿Y tú quién eres?
Ee too kee-ehn eh-rehs?

✻

Italian
Chi sei?
Kee say?

✻

German
Wer bist du?
Vair bisst doo?

✻

Welsh
Pwy wyt ti?
Poy owitee?

✻

Swedish
Vem är du?
Vem aer doo?

✻

Dutch
Wie ben jij?
Wee ben yey?

'What do you want for breakfast?'

French
Qu'est-ce que tu veux pour le petit déj?
Kas kuh too veuh pour luh petee dej?

*

Spanish
¿Qué quieres desayunar?
Keh kee-eh-rehs dehs-ah-yoo-nahr?

*

Italian
Che cosa vuoi per colazione?
Ke ko-za voo-oee payr ko-latseeo-nay?

*

German
Was willst du zum Frühstück?
Vass villst doo zumm froo-shtook?

*

Danish
Hvad vil du have til morgenmad?
Va vil doo hey te mornma?

*

Finnish
Mitä sä haluat aamupalaksi?
Mita sa halooat aamoopalaksi?

Global Sex Fact

*The Geisha of Japan would not perform
fellatio as it was considered demeaning.*

134 *Sex In Every City*

French
Comment tu aimes tes œufs?
Common too ame tez euff?

Spanish
**¿Cómo quieres que te ponga
los huevos?**
*Koh-moh kee-eh-rehs keh teh pohn-gah
lohs goo-eh-bohs?*

Italian
Come ti piacciono le uova?
Ko-may tee peeacheeo-no lay wo-va?

German
Wie magst du deine Eier?
Vee margst doo dye-neuh ey-er?

Global Sex Fact

*A medical study conducted in Pennsylvania
has shown that having regular sex helps
to boost the immune system.*

French
Si, si, je connais ton nom.
See, see, juh connay ton nom.

✳

Spanish
Sé muy bien cómo te llamas.
Seh moo-ee bee-ehn koh-moh teh yah-mahs.

✳

Italian
Davvero, lo so il tuo nome.
Dav-vay-ro, lo so eel too-o no-may.

✳

German
Klar, ich weiss wie du heisst.
Clarr, ish vie-ss vee doo hyse-t.

✳

Czech
Já už vím, jak se jmenuješ.
Yaa oozh veem yak seh ymenooyesh.

Essential Vocabulary

Massage, *noun*

French ***massage***
Spanish ***masaje***
Italian ***massagio***
German ***Massage***

French
Dans mon pays on appelle ça 'la Gaule du Matin'.
Don mon pay on appell sa 'la gaul doo matan'.

*

Spanish
**En mi país lo llamamos 'empalmada
matutina'.**
Ehn mee pah-ees loh yah-mah-mohs 'ehm-pahl-mah-dah
mah-too-tee-nah'.

*

Italian
**Nel mio paese lo chiamiamo 'la gloria
del mattino'.**
Nayl mee-o pa-ay-say lo kia-meeamo 'la glo-reea
dayl mat-teeno'.

*

German
**In meinem Land nennen wir das elnen
'strahlenden Morgen'.**
In mye-nem land nen-nen veer das ine-en
'shtrah-lenden morgan'.

*

Russian
В мое́й стране́ это называ́ется 'Morning Glory' (у́треннее
сия́ние).

V mayey strane eta nazyvayetsa 'Morning Glory'
(ootrinniye siyanie).

French
À la même heure demain?
A la mem eur duhman?

✳

Spanish
¿Mañana a la misma hora?
Mah-nee-ah-nah ah la mees-mah oh-rah?

✳

Italian
Domani alla stessa ora?
Do-manee al-la stays-sa o-ra?

✳

German
Morgen um die gleiche Zeit?
Morgan oom dee glye-sheuh tsite?

✳

Swedish
Samma tid imorgon?
Samma teed imorron?

Global Sex Fact

The Kama Sutra *– a fifth-century Hindu instructional book on the art of lovemaking – was written by Mallanga Vatsyayana, a celibate Hindu aesthtetic.*

When Sex Gets Serious

French
Je t'aime.
Juh tame.

✳

Spanish
Te amo.
Teh ah-moh.

✳

Italian
Ti amo.
Tee a-mo.

✳

German
Ich liebe dich.
Ick lee-beuh dish.

✳

Swedish
Jag älskar dig.
Yaag aelskar dey.

✳

Welsh
Caru ti.
Cari tee.

French
Veux-tu m'épouser?
Veuh too mepoozay?

✳

Spanish
¿Quieres casarte conmigo?
Kee-eh-rehs kah-sahr-teh kohn-mee-goh?

✳

Italian
Vuoi sposarmi?
Voo-oee sposar-mee?

✳

German
Willst du mich heiraten?
Villst doo mish hy-erarten?

✳

Hindi
मुझसे शादी करोगी?
Male: Moojhse shaadi karogi?

मुझसे शादी करोगे?
Female: Moojhse shaadi karogei?

Global Sex Fact

*Roman prostitutes often painted
or gilded their nipples and breasts.*

French
Fuyons et marions-nous.
Fwee-on ay maree-on noo.

✳

Spanish
Fuguémonos.
Phoo-gheh-moh-nohs.

✳

Italian
Facciamo una fuga d'amore.
Facheea-mo oo-na foo-ga da-moray.

✳

German
Lass uns durchbrennen.
Lass unss dirkbrennan.

✳

Hebrew
בואי נברח ונתחתן.
Boyi nivrakh oo-nitkhaten.

Global Sex Fact

In ancient Egypt it was believed that the god Osiris created the world through an act of masturbation.

French
Où est la bijouterie la plus proche?
Oo eh la bijooteree la ploo prosh?

∗

Spanish
***¿Dónde está la joyería
más próxima?***
*Dohn-deh ehs-tah la hoh-yeh-ree-ah
mahs proh-xee-mah?*

∗

Italian
Dov'è il gioielliere più vicino?
Do-ve eel joey-ayl-leeay-ray peeyoo vee-cheeno?

∗

German
Wo ist der nächste Juwelier?
Vo isst dare neckster yoovelleeay?

∗

Korean
가장 가까운 보석상이 어디죠?
Ga-jang ga-ka-oon bo-seuk-ssang-i eu-di-jo?

Global Sex Fact

*Worldwide, the most common mode of
transmission of the HIV virus is through
heterosexual intercourse.*

French
Si je t'épouse est-ce que j'aurai un visa?
See juh tepooz eskuh jobte-en un visa?

✳

Spanish
¿Si me caso contigo me darán
un permiso de residencia?
See meh kah-soh kohn-tee-goh meh dah-rahn
oon pehr-mee-soh deh rreh-see-dehn-thee-ah?

✳

Italian
Se ti sposo, mi danno la carta verde?
Say tee spo-so, mee dan-no la kar-ta vayr-day?

✳

German
Wenn ich dich heirate, bekomme ich dann
eine Green Card?
Ven ish dish hyera-teuh, bekom-meuh ish dan
ine-euh green card?

✳

Thai
ถ้าฉันแต่งงานกับคุณ ฉันจะได้กรีนการ์ดหรือเปล่า
Taa chan daeng-ngan gap khoon,
chan ja dai green card rue blao?

French
Et si on se mariait? Ah, tu l'es déjà!
Ay see on suh mar-e-ay? Ah, too leh deja!

✳

Spanish
¡Cásate conmigo! Ah, ¿tú ya lo estás?
Kah-sah-teh kohn-mee-goh! Ah, too yah loh ehs-tahs?

✳

Italian
Sposiamoci! Ah, lo sei già?
Sposeea-mochee! Ah, lo say gee-a?

✳

German
Lass uns heiraten! Schade, du bist doch schon.
Lass uns hy-erarten! Scharder, doo biss-t dock shone.

✳

Dutch
Laten we gaan trouwen! O, ben je al getrouwd?
Lahten weuh gahn trouwen! Oh, ben yeuh al getrouwd?

Global Sex Fact

One sixteenth-century test for female fertility involved the insertion of a garlic clove into the vagina. If, after twelve hours had passed the woman's breath smelt of garlic, she was considered to be fertile.

French

***Pourquoi ne viendrais tu pas rencontrer mes parents
ce dimanche?***

*Pourkwah nuh viendray too pa roncontray may paron
suh Dimonsh?*

✱

Spanish

***¿Por qué no vienes este domingo
a conocer a mis padres?***

*Pohr keh noh bee-eh-nehs ehs-teh doh-meen-goh
ah koh-noh-thehr ah mees pah-drehs?*

✱

Italian

***Perchè non vieni a conoscere i miei
genitori questa domenica?***

*Payr-ke non veeay-nee a ko-noshay-ray ee meeay-ee
jaynee-toree kwe-sta domay-neeka?*

✱

German

***Warum kommst du nicht am Sonntag
mit zu meinen Eltern?***

*Varoom komst doo nisht am sontag
mit tsoo mye-nen eltern?*

✱

Danish

***Hvorfor tager du ikke med hjem og hilser
på mine forældre på søndag?***

*Vofor tair doo ik meh yem og hilser
paw meen f'reldre paw sernday?*

French
Devine quoi, mon chéri? Je suis enceinte!
Deveen kwoi, mon sheree? Juh sweez on-sent!

✳

Spanish
¿A que no sabes una cosa?
¡Estoy embarazada!
Ah keh noh sah-behs oo-nah koh-sah?
Ehs-toh-ee ehm-bah-rah-thah-dah!

✳

Italian
Indovina un po' tesoro, sono incinta!
Een-doveena oo-n po tay-soro, so-no een-cheenta!

✳

German
Weisst du was Liebling, ich bin schwanger!
Vie-sst doo vass leebling, ish bin sshvanger!

✳

Finnish
Arvaa mitä kulta, mä olen raskaana!
Arva mita kolta, ma la rasskaan!

Global Sex Fact

The word 'vagina' originates from the Latin word for 'sheath'.

When Sex Goes Bad

French
Il y a t'il des urgences à l'hôpital du coin?
Il ee a til dez urjons a lopeetal doo kwun?

✳

Spanish
***¿Tiene una sala de urgencias
el hospital de esta ciudad?***
*Tee-eh-neh oo-nah sah-lah deh oor-hehn-thee-ahs
ehl ohs-pee-tahl deh ehs-tah thee-oo-dahd?*

✳

Italian
C'è il pronto soccorso all'ospedale locale?
Che eel pron-to so-korso allospay-dalay lo-kalay?

✳

German
Hat das Krankenhaus hier eine Notaufnahme?
Hat das krankenhouse heer ine-euh notoufnah-meuh?

✳

Czech
Je v místní nemocnici pohotovost?
Ye v meestnyee nemotsnyitsi pohotovost?

French
Où est la pharmacie de garde?
Oo eh la farmasee duh garde?

∗

Spanish
***¿Dónde encuentro yo ahora
una farmacia de guardia?***
*Dohn-deh ehn-koo-ehn-troh yoh ah-oh-rah
oo-nah phahr-mah-thee-ah deh goo-ahrr-dee-ah?*

∗

Italian
Dov'è la farmacia notturna?
Do-ve la farma-cheea not-toorna?

∗

German
Wo ist die nächste Nachtapoteke?
Vo isst dee neckster nacktappotaker?

∗

Russian
Как мне найти́ ночну́ю апте́ку?
Kak mnie nayti natchnooyoo aptiekoo?

Global Sex Fact

*Athletes in ancient Greece were sometimes
made to wear penis sheaths made of lead
to suppress erections.*

'When you said you could do it all night, I didn't think you meant snore.'

French

Quand tu m'as dit que tu pouvais le faire toute la nuit, je ne pensais pas que tu parlais de ronfler.

Kon too ma dee kuh too pouvay luh fare toot la nwee, juh nuh ponsay pa kuh too parlay duh ronflay.

✳

Spanish

Cuando dijiste que podías hacerlo toda la noche, no creí que estuvieras pensando en roncar.

Koo-ahn-doh dee-hees-teh keh poh-dee-ahs ah-thehr-loh toh-dah la noh-cheh, noh kreh-ee keh ehs-too-bee-eh-rahs pehn-sahn-doh ehn rrohn-kahr.

✳

Italian

Quando mi hai detto di poterlo fare tutta la notte, non pensavo che intendessi russare.

Kwan-do mee aee dayt-to dee potayr-lo fa-ray toot-ta la not-tay, non payn-savo ke een-tayn-days-see roos-saray.

✳

German

Als du sagtest, du könntest es die ganze Nacht machen, dachte ich nicht, dass du vom Schnarchen redest.

Als doo saagtest, doo keuntest es dee gantse nakht makhen, dakhte ish nisht, das doo fom shnarshen redest.

'Unfortunately, I can still see you through this blindfold.'

French
***Malheureusement, je peux toujours te voir
à travers le bandeau.***
*Maleureusuhmon, juh peuh toojour tuh vwoir
a trav-air luh bandoh.*

*

Spanish
***Por desgracia, sigo viéndote
a través de la venda en los ojos.***
*Pohr dehs-grah-thee-ah, see-goh vee-ehn-doh-teh
ah trah-behs deh la behn-dah ehn lohs oh-hohs.*

*

Italian
***Purtroppo, posso ancora vederti attraverso
questa benda.***
*Poor-trop-po, pos-so an-kora vaydayr-tee at-travay-rso
kwe-sta bayn-da.*

*

German
Leider sehe, ich dich noch durch diese Augenbinde.
Lie-deh zayer, ish dish nock dursh deezer owgun-bin-deh.

*

Hebrew
לצערי, אני יכול עדיין לראות אותך דרך כיסוי העיניים
הזה.
*Le-tsa'ari, ani yakhol adayn lirot otakh derekh kisui
ha-eynayim ha-ze.*

French
T'as commencé?
Ta commonsay?

✳

Spanish
¿Ya has empezado?
Yah ahs ehm-peh-thah-doh?

✳

Italian
Hai già iniziato?
Aee jeea eenee-zeeato?

✳

German
Hast du schon angefangen?
Hast doo shon aan-ge-faang-en?

✳

Hindi
तुमने शुरू कर दिया क्या?
Toomne shooroo kar diya kya?

Global Sex Fact

Patagonian Indians use a guesquel during intercourse – a ring-shaped device fashioned from mule's hair. Worn around the penis, it is said to produce intense orgasms in women.

French
*Où se trouve le centre de dépistage des MST
le plus proche?*
Oo suh troove luh sontruh duh daypistaje des em-es-teh
luh ploo prosh?

✳

Spanish
*¿Por dónde se va a la clínica
de enfermedades de transmisión
sexual?*
Pohr dohn-deh seh bah ah la clee-nee-kah
deh ehn-phehr-meh-dah-dehs deh trahns-mee-see-ohn
sehk-soo-ahl?

✳

Italian
Dov'è il centro MST?
Do-ve eel chen-tro em-me es-se tee?

✳

German
Wo ist die Geschlechtskrankheitenklinik?
Vo isst dee guhsshlektscrankheightenclineek?

✳

Welsh
Lle mae'r clinig heintiau rhywiol?
Chlay myer clinic hentee-ai chliwiol?

✳

Hebrew
מהי הדרך למרפאה למחלות מין?
Mahi-ha-derekh la-marpaa le-makhalot min?

French
Ça ne m'étais jamais arrivé avant.
Sa nuh metay jamay areevay avon.

✳

Spanish
Esto no me había pasado nunca.
Ehs-toh noh meh ah-bee-ah pah-sah-doh noon-kah.

✳

Italian
Questo non era mai successo prima.
Kwe-sto non e-ra ma-ee soo-ches-so pree-ma.

✳

German
Das ist mir nie passiert.
Dass isst meer nee passee-ert.

✳

Korean
전에 이런 일 전혀 없었어요.
Jeun-e ih-reun-il jeun-hyeu eup-sseut-sseu-yo.

Essential Vocabulary

Orgy, *noun*

French ***orgie***
Spanish ***orgìa***
Italian ***orgia***
German ***Orgie***

French
C'est tout?
Seh too?

∗

Spanish
¿Ya está?
Yah ehs-tah?

∗

Italian
Tutto qui?
Toot-o kwee?

∗

German
Ist das alles?
Ist dass alless?

∗

Russian
И́ это всё?
Ee eta vsio?

Global Sex Fact

It was common practice for an Athenian woman to rub cedar oil on her cervix as a method of contraception.

French
Ça, c'est un vilain eczéma.
Sa, set un vilan exzema.

✳

Spanish
Vaya sarpullido más feo.
Bah-yah sahrr-poo-yee-doh mahs pheh-oh.

✳

Italian
Che brutta eruzione cutanea.
Ke broot-ta eroo-tseeo-nay koo-tanaya.

✳

German
Das ist ein übeler Ausschlag.
Dass issed eyen oobeller owsshlarg.

✳

Dutch
Wat een nare uitslag.
Waht eun nahre ouwtslag.

Essential Vocabulary

Nipple, *noun*

French **mamelon, bout de sein**
Spanish **pezón**
Italian **capezzolo**
German **Nippel**

French
Essaye encore, je me fais plus d'effet tout seul / toute seule.
Essay onkore, juh muh fay ploo deffay too seul / toot seule.

✳

Spanish
***¡Ponle más ganas! Me lo hago mejor
por mi cuenta.***
*Pohn-leh mahs gah-nahs! Meh loh ah-goh meh-hohr
pohrr mee koo-ehn-tah.*

✳

Italian
***Impegnati di più, posso fare meglio
da solo / sola.***
*Eempay-neeatee dee peeyoo, pos-so fa-ray me-lyo
da so-lo / so-la.*

✳

German
Streng dich mehr an, das kann ich besser selber.
Shtreng dish mehr an, das kan ish besser selber.

✳

Hebrew
תתאמץ יותר, לבד הייתי מצליחה יותר.
Titamets yoter, levad hayiti matslikha yoter.

'The condom's split!'

French
Le préservatif s'est déchiré!
Luh prezervateef seh desheeray!

∗

Spanish
¡El condón se ha roto!
Ehl kohn-dohn seh ah rroh-toh!

∗

Italian
Il preservativo si è lacerato!
Eel pray-sayrva-teevo see eh lache-rato.

∗

German
Der Kondom hat gerissen!
Dare kon-dome hat guhrissen!

∗

Danish
Kondomet sprang!
Kondomme sprang!

Essential Vocabulary

Vibrator, *noun*

French **vibromasseur**
Spanish **vibrador**
Italian **vibratore**
German **Vibrator**

French

Est-ce que tu aimes mon corps?
Avant, j'étais un homme.
Eskuh too ame mon corps?
Avon, jetay un omme.

✲

Spanish

¿Te gusta mi cuerpo?
Antes era un hombre.
Teh goos-tah mee koo-ehrr-poh?
Ahn-tehs eh-rah oon ohm-brreh.

✲

Italian

Ti piace il mio corpo? Prima ero un uomo.
Tee peea-che eel mee-o kor-po? Pree-ma e-ro oo-n wo-mo.

✲

German

Gefall ich dir? Ich war einmal ein Mann.
Guhfal ish deer? Ish varr inemarl ine man.

✲

Finnish

Eikö ole aika hyvä kroppa mulla?
Noin entiseksi mieheksi.
Eyko ola euka hoova kroppo moolla?
Neun endeseksi miyeheksi.

'What? You only have two each in your country?'

French
Quoi? Vous en avez que deux chacun dans votre pays?
Kwoi? Vooz on avay kuh deuh shackun don votruh pay?

Spanish
***¿Cómo? ¿En tu país sólo tenéis
dos por cabeza?***
*Koh-moh? Ehn too pah-ees soh-loh teh-neh-ees
dohs pohr kah-beh-thah?*

Italian
***Cosa? Nel tuo paese ne avete solo
due ciascuno / ciascuna?***
*Ko-za? Nayl too-o pa-ay-say nay avay-tay so-lo
doo-e cheea-skoono / cheea-skoona?*

German
Was? Man hat nur zwei in deinem Land?
Vass? Man hat nurr z-vie in dye-nem lant?

Czech
U vás máte kaẅdá jen dvě?
Oo vaas maate kazhda yen dvye?

French

Désolé, je croyais t'avoir prévenu que je n'en étais qu'à la moitié du processus de changement de sexe.

Dezolay, juh crwoyay tavwoir prayvenoo kuh je non etay ka la mwahte-ay doo prosesoo duh shonjemon duh sex.

Spanish

Perdona, creía que ya te había dicho que todavía me falta la otra mitad de la operación de cambio de sexo.

Pehr-doh-nah, kreh-ee-ah keh yah teh ah-bee-ah dee-choh keh toh-dah-bee-ah meh phahl-tah la oh-trah mee-tahd deh la oh-peh-rah-thee-ohn deh kahm-bee-oh deh sehk-soh.

Italian

Scusami, credevo di averti detto di non aver completato ancora l'intervento chirurgico di cambiamento di sesso.

Skooza-mee, kre-dayvo dee avayr-tee dayt-to dee non avayr komplay-tato an-kora leentayr-vaynto keeroor-jeeko dee kambeea-maynto dee ses-so.

German

Ich dachte, ich hätte erwähnt, dass meine Geschlechtsumwandlung noch nicht beendet ist.

Ish dakhte, ish het-te er-vaynt, das mye-neuh geshleshts-oomvandloong nokh nisht be-endet ist.